MW01235339

THE MISOGYNY FACTOR

ANNE SUMMERS is a writer, journalist, editor of the digital magazine *Anne Summers Reports* and author, whose latest books are *The Lost Mother* and *On Luck*. She is author of the renowned *Damned Whores and God's Police*. She writes for a number of publications including the *Sydney Morning Herald*, *The Age* and the *Australian Financial Review*. She has worked as a senior bureaucrat and political adviser, and is the former editor-in-chief of the landmark feminist New York based *Ms.* magazine. Anne has a PhD from the University of Sydney and honorary doctorates from the University of New South Wales and Flinders University. In 1989 she was made an Officer of the Order of Australia for her services to journalism and to women. In 2011 she, along with three other leading feminists, was honoured by Australia Post by having her image placed on a postage stamp.

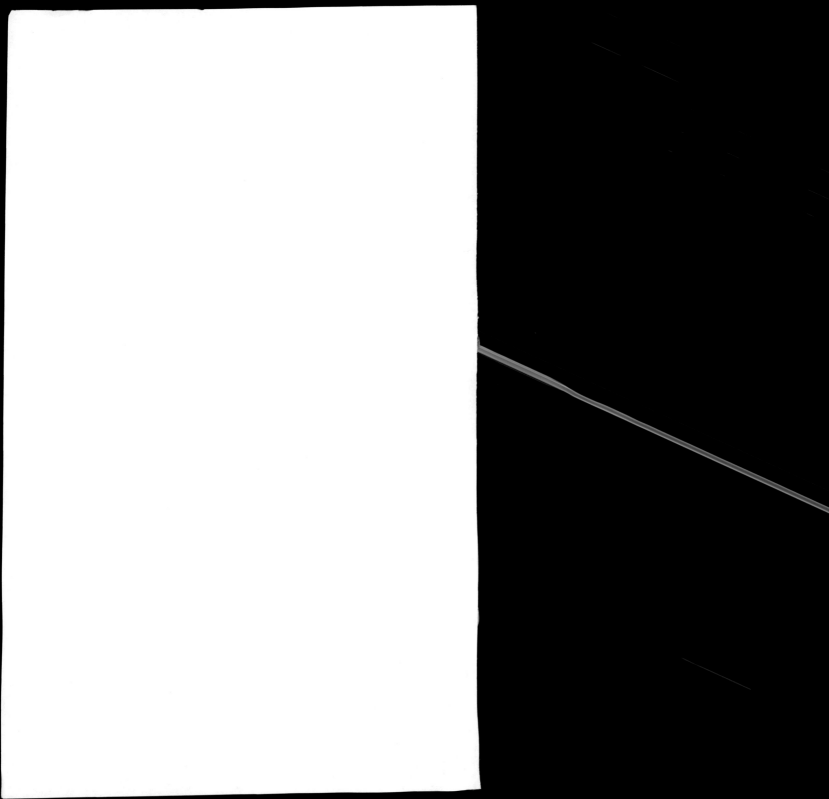

THE
MISOGYNY
FACTOR

ANNE SUMMERS

NEWSOUTH

A NewSouth book
Published by
NewSouth Publishing
University of New South Wales Press Ltd
University of New South Wales
Sydney NSW 2052
AUSTRALIA
newsouthpublishing.com

National Library of Australia Cataloguing-in-Publication entry
 Author: Summers, Anne, 1945– author.
 Title: The misogyny factor/Anne Summers.
 ISBN: 9781742233840 (paperback)
 ISBN: 9781742241456 (epub/mobi)
 ISBN: 9781742246390 (ePDF)
 Notes: Includes index.
 Subjects: Misogyny – Australia.
 Women – Political activity – Australia.
 Women executives – Australia
 Women – Australia – Social conditions.
 Women – Australia – Economic conditions.
 Dewey Number: 305.40994

Design Avril Makula
Cover design Sandy Cull, gogoGingko
Printer Griffin

This book is printed on paper using fibre supplied from plantation or
sustainably managed forests.

UNSW
AUSTRALIA

'Moll!'

– female interjector yelling at
Prime Minister Julia Gillard from the
public gallery of Parliament House during
Question Time, 12 March 2013

Contents

Acknowledgments

This book initially grew out of two speeches I delivered in 2012: the Fraser Oration in Canberra in July 2012 and the University of Newcastle Human Rights and Social Justice Lecture in August 2012. I am deeply indebted to the people who invited me to give these speeches: Andrew Leigh, the federal member for Fraser in the ACT; and Kevin McConkey, Deputy Vice Chancellor (Academic and Global Relations) at the University of Newcastle. I am also grateful to Professor Louise Chappell at the University of New South Wales, and Tanja Farman and Bec Dean from Performance Space at CarriageWorks who each invited me to re-present 'Her Rights at Work' (what is now known as 'The Newcastle

Speech') to new audiences and thus have a further opportunity to gauge reaction to my arguments. I delivered variants on the speeches to other audiences and appreciate the opportunities to do so that were offered by Professor Caroline S. Taylor of Edith Cowan University, Laura Stokes of TEDxSouthBankWomen and the Australian Services Union National Conference.

It was Kathy Bail's idea to turn the Fraser Oration into a book; I suggested she might like to consider my including the (yet-to-be-delivered) Newcastle speech as well. I thank Kathy and the rest of the team at NewSouth Publishing for their snappy work in so speedily getting this book published and known about out there in the world: Phillipa McGuinness, Heather Cam and Matt Howard.

Once I started turning the speeches into a book, I soon discovered there were many things I did not know, or needed to check, and I thank the following people who all helped me do this: Ashley Hogan, Tracy Howe and Taryn Champion from New South Wales Women's Refuge Movement, Ruth Medd from Women on Boards, Mary Ann O'Loughlin, Julianne Schultz, Emma-Kate Symons, Nareen Young and Janet Wilson.

And for being there for me in all kinds of way, a big thank you to Jane Caro, Anne de Salis, Marion Hosking, Ged Kearney, Sally McManus and Jenna Price. Most of all, to Chip Rolley for his never-ending support and love.

Introduction

Once, if a newspaper or magazine wanted to sell extra copies, it would put a banner headline 'What Do Women Want?' on the front page. These days, the attention-grabber is 'Can Women Have It All?'

We've come a long way, baby.

If once we were vapid creatures who, in the view of Sigmund Freud, could not decide what we wanted, now we are voracious careerists who want the lot. That the question is even posed is, of course, gratuitous and demeaning, since the 'all' refers to having a job and a family. If you are a bloke, you can have it 'all' without anyone raising an eyebrow – or even asking how you manage to 'do it all'.

This was a source of particular irritation to Nicola Roxon who unexpectedly resigned as Australia's first woman attorney-general in early February 2013 and who announced her intention to leave the parliament at the election to be held in September 2013 because she wants to be at home for her young daughter. She often mentioned in media interviews that it really riled her that she was constantly asked how she managed to combine being a Cabinet minister with being a wife and mother, whereas her male colleagues who were husbands and fathers were never asked the same question.

It is not just frustrating but, in fact, scandalous that the myriad assumptions and, let's face it, prejudices that lie behind this question have not really altered in more than half a century. If we didn't still think, deep down, that women's primary function is to breed and raise children, the question of 'all' simply would not arise.

If we truly accepted the proposition that women and men are equal, and equally entitled to enjoy having a family and having a job, we wouldn't be wasting our time having this conversation.

Instead, we'd perhaps be telling our kids about the bad old days before the harmonisation of work, family and school. We'd be rolling our eyes at the memory of school holidays that were out of sync with parental holidays, and at the way school finished hours before the end of the office day, leaving parents at their wits' end sorting out how to cope.

Craziest of all, we'd recall, was how childcare had been seemingly designed by a sadist who expected mothers – yes, you wouldn't believe it, but it was the mums who had to do it back then – to drop kids off on their way to work and then hightail it back through peak-hour traffic to pick them up before the centre closed. As for what it all cost, well, women would tell their incredulous offspring, I practically worked for nothing by the time I paid childcare fees.

The kids would be amazed to hear that a society that was supposed to be managed by economic rationalists had been unable to figure out that enabling women to get into the full-time workforce in the same proportions as men would increase gross domestic product by 13 per cent (and this was after all the services needed to support women's employment – childcare and so on – had been purchased).

There'd be other horror stories to tell, but by now the kids would be bored by accounts of the olden days when society was so, well, stupid. They take utterly for granted that both women and men can 'have it all', because that's the natural state of affairs, and society is organised around ensuring that it all works smoothly and equitably.

And it is precisely because we in Australia are not having this conversation that I decided to write this book. We are fumbling around the edges of the issues, tinkering with policies, doing quick fixes but never sitting back and saying: *What exactly do we need to do to ensure our society promotes equality and makes it possible for women, as well as men, to live the lives they want?*

℃℧

Some societies are well on their way to doing this. They tend to be in Europe. Perhaps surprisingly, countries such as France, that we might have viewed as rather conservative when it came to gender matters, have worked out a way for women to combine having both fertility and workforce participation rates that far outstrip ours. As far as I know, there is no talk of 'having it all' in France. They just get on with it.

In Australia a surprisingly large number of us are censorious towards women who don't conform to our (impossible) ideals. Many would prefer women with children to stay home (they can worry later about losing their skills and their confidence and their super), or if they insist on combining motherhood with having a job, these people expect them to be totally stressed-out all the time. That'll teach you, they seem to be saying.

Then there's the women who have had the temerity to forge successful careers and neglected to have children. Our two leading female politicians, Julia Gillard and Julie Bishop, are both alternately castigated and pitied for being in this category – not for not 'having it all' but for choosing a different path. And seeming pretty damned satisfied with their choices, too.

Most tragic of all is the fact that we are still having this conversation in 2013. In February this year it was a full 50 years since the publication of Betty Friedan's *The Feminine*

Mystique, the landmark book that chronicled the dissatis-
faction of those highly educated, middle-class American
women who were fulfilling what was then considered to be
their female destiny as full-time wives and mothers. There
was no question whatsoever of them 'having it all' – and it
was driving them crazy. Friedan's book helped give rise to
the modern Women's Movement, which urged that women
have the right to a larger range of choices in how they lived
their lives and equal rights with men to pursue their dreams.

Back then, all the talk was about how to break down
the barriers that had kept women out of the workforce,
and all the other places they wanted to be. It was about
redesigning our lives so women could be everywhere ('A
woman's place is in the House. And the Senate' was an
early slogan) and do everything. No one thought for a
minute that it would not be possible, once the legal barriers were removed.

And it was – for a decade or so. It wasn't until the 1980s
that the backlash began and women were suddenly being
told not just that they couldn't 'have it all' but that, actually, they didn't want it. Suddenly it was too hard, too
stressful. The long march backwards had begun.

In August 2012 I delivered a speech at the University
of Newcastle documenting the vilification of Prime Minister Julia Gillard and arguing that if she were an ordinary
worker, she would have a case for sex discrimination and
sexual harassment. This speech attracted an extraordinary
response and was read by many thousands; the response

suggested that there was widespread disquiet at the way Australia's first female Prime Minister was being disparaged by the Opposition, by the media and by many ordinary citizens. The Newcastle speech followed one I'd given a few months earlier, the Fraser Oration in Canberra, where I had tried to account for what had gone wrong with our quest for equality between the sexes in Australia. This little book combines the ideas of these two speeches, together with my account of the extraordinary events of 2012, and presents an argument about why we still fall so far short of our stated goal of equality. The reason, I maintain, is 'the misogyny factor'.

The year 2012 was probably the best year for Australian women since 1972. Back then, the newly emerged and still energised Women's Movement presented its plan for women's equality to the newly elected Whitlam Government in Canberra – and found itself being taken seriously. Forty years on, the reforms begun in 1972 seemed to have faltered and women once again found themselves impatient for change. 2012 was the year when women decided they'd had enough of the insults, the inequality and the indignities they had endured for too long. It was a year of activism. It was the year of 'Destroying the Joint', of #everydaysexism, of outpourings of rage and grief over raped and murdered young women in Melbourne and Delhi, of the first female Prime Minister of this country standing up in federal parliament and denouncing sexism and misogyny. It was quite a year.

Because of these events, women – especially young women – were more receptive than they'd been for a long time to hearing the facts of their situation. Online publications such as *Women's Agenda* and *Daily Life* started up and provided daily articles on the many facets of being a woman in Australia today, including presenting some of the distressing facts, such as lack of equal pay or the increases in violence against women. Women, too, took to Twitter and Facebook and their own blogs and other outlets to describe their lives and to comment on where they felt they were being short-changed.

This is the context for this book.

It is a short and, at times, angry look at the forces that are standing in the way of women's equality. I nominate three indicators of the success we have yet to achieve: inclusion, equality and respect. Until women are included in all areas of our society, until we are treated equally and with respect once we are there, we will not have succeeded in what I call the equality project.

I nominate the misogyny factor as *the* obstacle. Briefly, the misogyny factor is that set of attitudes and entrenched practices that are embedded in most of our major institutions (business, politics, the military, the media, the church, academia) that stand in the way of women being included, treated equally and accorded respect. In making this case, I am not sidetracked by strict dictionary definitions of 'misogyny'. Sure, it can mean, 'hatred of women' and we still see far too many instances of that. But it is more complicated, and far more widespread than the prejudices of individuals, which is why I use the term 'the misogyny factor'. So I am not distracted by absurd propositions such as: so-and-so can't be misogynist because he is married, has daughters, has a mother, and so on. I am talking about systemic beliefs and behaviour, which are predicated on the view that women do not have the fundamental right to be part of society beyond the home. It is entirely possible for a man to have women in his life and yet hold such prejudicial attitudes – and plenty do. They are often sugar-coated with diversionary discussions about motherhood or merit, the two major excuses for excluding women, but deep-down they are simply old-fashioned atavistic attitudes. These people believe that, once they are mothers, women just do not belong in the world outside the home. They also tend to have the conviction that all women *ought* to be mothers and, therefore, confined to the domestic sphere. Such views can be, and are, held by women as well as men. Sometimes women argue them to justify their own situation, but there are plenty of examples of women who are in the wider corporate or business world doing so as well. Why they defend misogyny is mystifying, yet plenty of women do.

Sexism goes hand in hand with misogyny. Sexism provides the rationale for misogyny. It is the set of attitudes towards women that justifies their exclusion, their being treated as inferiors and their being denied respect. Sexism, like racism, ascribes attributes to people on the basis of a single inherited and unmutable characteristic – a person's sex or their race – without regard to their individuality, and is then used as the basis for treating them differently and unfavourably. So when a woman is dismissed as 'weak' or 'hysterial' or 'emotional' or 'aggressive' or 'a bitch', her detractor is drawing on a repertoire of stereotypes about women that supposedly typecast the entire sex and are then seen as justification for discriminating against them. It's a classic double-bind. Women's behaviour is deemed to be predetermined by sexual stereotypes, which are then used as the prism through which to judge (and condemn) them. If misogyny is the theory of women's inferiority and unworthiness and, therefore, unsuitability to be equal players in our society, sexism is the everday expression of it.

This book is not anti-male, nor is it intended that only women should read it. I hope men will and I hope that they will agree with my arguments. Men, more than women, are the gate-keepers and we won't change the world without you. Indeed, we'd like your help.

This book is short and it is focused. It does not pretend to cover every relevant aspect of women's lives in Australia today. I don't deal with health or housework, with race or religion, with sexuality or stilettos. I deal mostly with economic facts. I denounce the fact that there is a million-dollar penalty to being a young woman in Australia today. My starting point is the absurdity of a society predicated on a double standard: men can be fulfilled as fathers and as workers, yet we still argue the toss about whether women can 'have it all'. And, increasingly we conclude, no they can't, and they shouldn't, and they better not. And, guess what, the statistics show they aren't. And so I decry the low rate, compared with other industrialised countries, of women's workforce participation, especially of women with children. This is bad for the nation – we can measure the economic benefits foregone – and it also penalises women financially and in other ways. I also despair at the high and increasing rates of violence against women in this country.

Most of all, I try to lay out the case for how the misogyny factor is denying women inclusion, equality and respect. And why we need to fight against it.

1

The Misogyny Factor

It is Australia Day, 2013. This is the day when the nation puts itself on show, puffs out its chest and says: this is who we are. It is a day of citizenship ceremonies, when recent arrivals officially join our ranks, a day when we have barbecues and parties and all kinds of official events to celebrate our nationhood. It is also the day when large numbers of people are honoured by the government for their service to the community, and it is the day after we have learned who has been selected as 'Australian of the Year'. On Australia Day we show our face to the world, and to ourselves, and reveal what kind of country we really are. And that face, it turns out, is mostly male.

On 26 January 2013 Order of Australia honours were awarded to 571 people, 425 of them men and only 146 women. Just 25.5 per cent of these awards went to women. Not a single woman received the AC (the Companion of the Order of Australia), the highest of the honours, and the percentage of women honoured overall was one of the lowest on record. The night before, the magazine editor and publisher Ita Buttrose was named 'Australian of the Year'. She was the first woman for eight years and just the fourth woman in 20 years to have received this honour. In its first 31 years, until 1993 when the timing of the award was changed and no appointment made that year, it was somewhat fairer: between 1961 and 1992 seven women had been 'Australian of the Year', eight if you included Judith Durham, a band member of The Seekers, who were collectively named 'Australian of the Year' in 1967.[1] This is just one of many examples in Australia today of women's representation in the organisations and institutions that define our country being not just low but lower than it used to be back when we seemed to take women's equality a bit more seriously.

How can this be? It is, after all, well over a hundred years after Australian women[2] got the right to vote, and more than forty years since Gough Whitlam put equality of the sexes on the national agenda by promising in his campaign election speech, delivered on 13 November 1972, that his government would introduce anti-discrimination legislation and equal pay for women.

It seemed a simple goal. It was easy to outline what needed to happen: legal and other barriers to equality needed to be removed, measures to promote equality needed to be put in place, and women's particular needs recognised. Anti-discrimination laws would be a key tool to remove impediments to equality. Women would be given equal access to education, jobs and remuneration. They would be able to exercise reproductive control by having access to contraception and abortion. And, of course, childcare and other essential supports would be provided to enable them to combine participating in the paid workforce with having children. Equality would be all about ending the traditional view that women's only place was in the home, and promoting the alternative notion that women should participate fully in all areas of society. How hard would that be?

Extremely hard, as it turned out.

Forty years on we are not even close to achieving equality. It really is quite absurd when you think about it. Why is it that in forty years we have not been able to bring about a series of changes that are logical, rational, just and, as well as being personally beneficial to women themselves, would be of tremendous economic advantage to the nation?

Certainly it was an ambitious goal. In order for it to happen there needed to be a radical restructure of virtually all of our institutions in order to reform the old, unequal basis on which most of them were conceived and operated. It meant taking on and challenging, as a prelude to reform, entrenched attitudes and practices that were predicated on the idea that women had no legitimate role outside the domestic sphere. It meant confronting these attitudes – these prejudices – in major institutions of society such as business, the media, the military, and the church. It also meant trying to end decades, if not centuries, of privilege that were founded on the inequality of the sexes and which would be threatened by the large-scale entry of women into these organisations and institutions. There were clear national economic benefits, as well as individual ones, to be gained.

In the past, we have embraced huge, ambitious projects for national betterment. How ambitious, for instance, was it to reroute several rivers, flood a few towns and create a massive hydro project that would generate electricity and provide irrigation waters to parched farmland across half our continent? The Snowy Mountains Scheme was just that: logical, rational, just and of tremendous economic advantage to the nation. We managed to complete that in just 25 years.

But while we are good at engineering such huge national construction projects – think also of the Overland Telegraph and, currently, the National Broadband Network – perhaps we are not so adept when it comes to engineering social projects. In fact, we don't even like to think of equality between the sexes in such terms. We – or many of us – would prefer to talk about rights and fairness and entitlements. I want to argue here that such talk has not achieved what we want and maybe it is time to take another approach.

The question I explore in this book is: Why have we Australians denied ourselves the benefits of equality? We know that increasing women's workforce participation adds substantially to national economic growth, as well as providing financial benefits and personal fulfilment to women themselves. So why have we been so irrational as to forego the economic and other advantages that would stem from having a truly equal society? And why, when it comes to equality of the sexes, have we seemingly laid aside our long-standing concerns for social justice? Australia has a long and proud tradition of pioneering reforms that have granted or improved upon political, social and economic rights for her citizens. Australia created the secret ballot to prevent corruption in elections. Australia led the world with many reforms designed to end the exploitation of workers and to improve society for everyone: it was the first to introduce the eight-hour day, recognising that workers were entitled to leisure as well as rest after their labour; Australia introduced conciliation and arbitration processes for fairly determining wages and settling disputes between workers and employers. Australia was one of the first places in the world to grant women the right to vote (the states of South Australia and Western Australia enfranchised women in

1894 and 1899, respectively, before national suffrage was introduced in 1901). We were the first to introduce such reforms as child endowment, the widow's pension, and policewomen. Why, with such an innovative history, have we fallen so short with women's equality?

Why is it that despite at least forty years of legislative and other measures designed to achieve equality, women are still paid considerably less than men, women are still seen as having the primary responsibility for raising children, women's workforce participation rate lags behind men's and the top ranks of our major organisations are still, overwhelmingly, male? Why haven't our anti-discrimination laws eradicated this inequality? Why haven't decades of agitation and activism by women, and the men who support them, led us to our goal? What we wanted seemed to be so self-evidently necessary and fair that we found it hard to imagine that we could fail. We thought it was going to be simple: a matter of a few laws, a lot of persuasion, perhaps a little bit of enforcement. What has gone wrong? Why have we failed?

My years of thinking, writing and acting on the many issues surrounding women's equality have led to me to conclude the following: in pursuing the strategy we did, we failed to take into account that it was not just a matter of legislating to prevent discrimination against women. We did not realise that it wasn't just a case of challenging the sexist assumptions that women should remain locked in traditional roles. We were, perhaps understandably but in retrospect naively, unwilling to admit that there was actual opposition to the very idea of equality. Not everyone agrees that women and men should be equal. We saw this dramatically on display when the Sex Discrimination Act was first introduced into federal parliament in late 1983; the opposition to it was ferocious, with people claiming it would destroy the family, strip women of their femininity and all kinds of other ludicrous claims. We underestimated the extent of the actual resistance. And the strength of the forces that were going to do everything they could to prevent women from having an equal role in our Australian society. In short, we failed to fully understand the misogyny factor.

We can see it clearly now. It has always been there, we realise, but we thought it would diminish over time. We thought our arguments would prevail. We perhaps thought that people would just get used to the fact that women were everywhere, doing all kinds of jobs. We thought that our continued presence would permeate into acceptance, maybe grudging at first, but gradually approving, even welcoming. Not so.

On 29 January, the ABC's opinion and news analysis website *The Drum* ran a poll that asked the following question: *146 women, compared to 425 men, received Australia Day honours. Do we need a new system to ensure parity?* By 31 January when the poll was taken down, 2934 people had voted. The results were confronting: 59 per cent had voted 'No' and only 41 per cent 'Yes'.[3] This poll was conducted on the same day as *The Drum* published my article about the extraordinary bias against women in the Order of Australia Honours system.[4] So those who voted against there being parity in our nation's honours were not doing so in ignorance of the fact that women are awarded only a tiny fraction of these awards. We can only conclude those people agree with the bias, that they do not want equality of the sexes in this country, or perhaps they do not value highly the contribution women make to the nation. This is the misogyny factor clearly on show.

I had documented the fact that only 30 per cent of awards had gone to women since they had been established by the Whitlam government in 1975 (replacing the old imperial honours system of Knights and Dames, OBEs and CBEs). As we have seen, the 2013 Australia Day honours fell short even of that low benchmark, with only 25 per cent of the awards going to women. But what was even worse, I argued, was the distribution of the awards. Of the 7645 women who received Order of Australia honours between 1975 and 2010, only 0.73 per cent were awarded the highest honour, the AC (Companion of the Order of Australia); just 4.26 per cent got the next one down, the AO (Officer of the Order of Australia); 19.4 per cent were awarded an AM (Member of the Order of Australia), while the rest – a full 75.6 per cent of all women who have ever been 'gonged' for service to their country – had to be content with the lowest-ranking honour, the OAM (Medal of the Order of Australia).[5] The comparable statistic for the

17,917 men who were honoured over the same period are: AC – 1.84 per cent; AO – 8.95 per cent; AM 29.26 per cent; OAM – 59.95 per cent. This is a stark demonstration of the misogyny factor at work. Here is continuing and, on the 2013 figures, worsening, institutional bias against women in the honours list that demonstrates who we as a nation rank as having best served our country. When it comes to deciding what kind of service is most meritorious, women and their work are devalued in cruelly unambiguous terms.

If we understand that it is the misogyny factor standing in the way of equality of the sexes, then perhaps we will be able to fight it more effectively. Naming something, and understanding how it operates is the start of the process of changing it. Observing it in action, documenting its insidious effects, laying it out for all to see, means we can no longer pretend that we just need to be patient, or more polite, or more clever, and things will eventually change. We have clung to that belief for forty years and where has it got us? It's time to stop asking nicely for what is rightfully ours. It's time to demand equality. And that means confronting, head-on, the continuing and entrenched bias – some of it exhibited in actual hatred – towards women in this country. It means taking on the misogyny factor.

Put simply, the misogyny factor is the entrenched, institutionalised resistance to women's equality. The misogyny factor encompasses the concept of 'misogyny', a term traditionally defined as the hatred of women, but it is broader than that. In today's 21st-century Australia, where we have had at least a century of women struggling to engage fully in public life (fighting for the right to vote, to stand for parliament, to enter the paid workforce, to be paid the same wages as men and so on), the misogyny factor is a more complex and sophisticated set of responses than can be explained by mere hatred. The misogyny factor is manifested in the public and private institutions that run our country and which have proved extraordinarily resistant to having women exercise real power within their ranks. These institutions, and the individuals who run them, don't necessarily hate women, they just don't want women around, at least not as peers and equals – and certainly not running the show. It is fine to have women as handmaidens (secretaries or personal assistants) or doing all those middle-ranking jobs in the offices and other workplaces around the country, but women are not welcome further up the ranks. There is no room at the top. The fact that Australia has a female Governor-General, a female Prime Minister and (a small number of) women in top positions in some institutions does not disprove what I am saying. In fact, as I will show, the fact that these few women have managed, against all odds, to make it to these top jobs has unleashed such an extraordinary torrent of hatred and hostility that it underscores my argument.

Misogyny is embedded in our way of life and always has been. We thought we were making inroads, changing these attitudes, introducing true partnerships between women and men but, we now know, we were wrong. The misogyny factor is the embodiment of resistance to the equal participation of women and men in our society. It is remarkably resilient and resistant to reason, to argument, to rationality, even to legal intervention. Simple commonsense ought to dictate that the economic benefits of equality to society and to individuals should trump misogyny. That has not been the case. Nor has the fact that many men advocate and fight for equality. The misogyny factor is not simply a case of men against women. It refers to a set of attitudes and behaviours that can just as easily be exhibited by women. The misogyny factor is not just men expressing bias or a desire to exclude women; many women actively support and perpetuate the system that prevents their sex from fully participating in all areas of society. Why these women act as apologists for their own oppression is mystifying; perhaps they think they will be treated as exceptions and, unlike other women, will not be spurned and demeaned. They forget that it is the exceptions that make the rule.

So my argument should not be seen as anti-male. It is not. And this book is not just for women. The misogyny factor is an entrenched system of attitudes and practices that are designed to exclude women, or to demean them if they do succeed in gaining entry. Not all those who perpetuate and benefit from the misogyny factor are men, and not all men benefit from it, but it is fair to say that the vast majority who do are men. Those men don't want to relinquish their power, or even to share it, and so they make it as difficult and as unpleasant as possible for those few women who manage to infiltrate their ranks. Misogyny is exemplified by the exclusion of women from exercising power in the non-domestic areas of our society: that is how hostility towards women is manifested in modern Australia and it is the misogyny factor that has been largely responsible for frustrating all our efforts to date to create a society where women can share real equality with men.

2

The Equality Project

In the wildly optimistic days of second-wave feminism in the 1970s, we drew up what was effectively a blueprint for equality. It laid out the principles, and then the steps we needed to take and the measures we had to put in place to achieve equality between the sexes in Australia. After its initial radicalism in the formation years of 1969 to 1971, the Australian Women's Movement, for the most part, opted for a pragmatic approach to change. The Movement seized upon the opportunity afforded by the election of the Whitlam government in 1972 to push for a realistic and achievable agenda. Many of us were aware that in doing so we were scaling back ('selling out'?) our formerly far more radical demands for women's liberation, something that would have involved a total transformation of society and of the roles of women and men. Equality was seen then as a short-term objective achievable principally through legislative and other government-supported measures that would be a mere stepping-stone on the road to liberation. Little did we realise just how difficult achieving what we thought was the more modest goal of equality would turn out to be.

We tried, we really did. We knew what we wanted – to liberate women from their traditional roles – and we thought we knew how to achieve it. But we are still not there. Some might say that, despite all that we have achieved, we are still not even close. So let's take a look at what we have done and then try to assess how far it has taken us.

The principles were straightforward: for women to be equal, they needed economic independence and the ability to control their fertility. It was very simple: women needed the financial ability to support themselves so they were not forced to be dependent on another person, most often a husband. That meant having a decent education so that a woman was equipped to get a job or embark on a career that would pay enough for her to be self-sufficient if she chose to be. Second, and just as important, a woman needed to be able to decide when and if she would have children. That meant she had to have reliable and affordable contraception and, in case that failed, resort to medically safe, legal and – again – affordable abortion. Without these two basics, women could not be in control of their lives. But, once you were able to support yourself financially, and to control your fertility, then the world was wide open to you. You had choices. You could pursue opportunities. You could decide when and if you wanted to start a family. As a pre-requisite to equality, women had to be able to make the same choices men could.

The first, and most basic, elements of our blueprint had to address how to implement these principles. This being Australia, where government has a big influence on the way we live, having a sympathetic government would be a key, probably essential, element to our success. In retrospect, this was probably one of the strategic errors of the early Women's Movement. We should have realised the need for a powerful external lobby organisation, as unions, farmers, miners and almost every industry group you can think of has, that would put pressure on government, research our situation and our needs, run advocacy and publicity campaigns, and generally represent the interests of women. Instead, we put our faith in government. Some of us actually went to work inside the system, persuading ourselves that we could make changes from within. And, on the outside, we relied on our own amateur persuasive efforts to influence the direction of policies that would foster women's equality. In fact, we considered ourselves blessed by history. At the very time the Women's Movement in Australia had pretty much figured out what needed to be done, the Whitlam government came to power with the promise to put women's equality high on its agenda. We pitied our American sisters who in 1972 had to endure the re-election of the decidedly women-unfriendly President Richard Nixon. Just a year earlier, he had famously vetoed a child-care bill, which was strongly supported by women's groups and which had been passed by both houses of Congress, on the grounds that it would represent the 'Sovietization of American children'.[1] By contrast, the second act of the Whitlam Government – the very first was to honour its undertaking to abolish conscription for military service – was to write to the Industrial Registrar of the Conciliation and Arbitration Commission seeking to reopen the case on equal pay so that the government could support it. (The previous government had opposed it.)

Over the past forty years, the responses of Australian governments to implementing the measures needed for women's equality – what I will now call 'the equality project' – have veered between strong support and more or less total opposition. Generally, Labor governments have been more supportive of the equality project and Coalition governments more likely to either stall progress or even wind back the clock. The result has been that our progress has been erratic. There has seldom, if ever, been bipartisan agreement even on the premise of women's equality, let alone on the basic steps required to achieve it.

In the 1970s it seemed self-evident that the way to achieve equality was to remove the legal and other barriers that prevented women from participating fully in society. If, for instance, a law stipulated that upon marriage women must resign from full-time employment in the public service, the teaching service or the banks, then it was obvious that that law should be repealed. (And, yes, there was such a law.) If a law enshrined women's wages at 59 per cent of what was paid to men, then another law ought to take its place and require that women receive 'equal pay for equal work'. The logical and most efficient way to deal with such legal inequalities was simply to enact laws that made it unlawful to discriminate on the grounds of sex or marital status. Such laws would not merely outlaw discrimination, and give women the ability to make complaints and receive remedies in the event of discrimination, but they would also require governments to remove all discrimination from all laws. (They could start by removing the male pronoun from all laws. And, eventually, they did just that.) Simple.

It was all so obvious. What could possibly go wrong?

It started out promisingly enough. The Whitlam Era (1972–75) was brief, yet it managed to set the parameters of the equality project. It began with its dramatic intervention into the equal pay case that resulted in the Arbitration Commission granting women 'equal pay for work of equal value'. Equally impressive was the government's decisive measures to help women control their fertility. Within days of being elected, the government had removed the 37.5 per cent tariff on imported rubber contraceptives, such as condoms and diaphragms, greatly reducing their cost. But of even greater symbolic value, and of immense practical help to women, was the removal of the 27.5 per cent 'luxury' tax on the contraceptive pill; it was also placed on the Pharmaceutical Benefits Scheme (PBS), bringing the price down to an affordable 50 cents a month. The federal government also, for the first time, provided funds to the Family Planning Association to enable it to expand its services. This was important because many doctors would only prescribe the pill to married women, whereas family planning services were mostly run by women who would not deny single women the tools (both the information and the contraceptives themselves) to control their fertility. Combined, these actions gave women unprecedented freedom and the consequent ability to make decisions about what to do with their lives.

In its few short years in office, the Whitlam government established many of the essential building blocks for equality: paid maternity leave was introduced for federal public servants; the Family Law Act was passed, allowing for no-fault divorce and establishing the Family Court; the government-funded childcare services that had been introduced by the previous government were given substantially increased funding; and money was made available for the women's services, such as health centres, family planning, refuges and rape crisis centres, that had very recently been established by the Women's Movement. A supporting mother's benefit was introduced that, for the first time, provided a regular source of income for single mothers. The government initiated anti-discrimination legislation but this was not passed due to the premature dismissal of the government. The position of Women's Advisor to the Prime Minister was created as an important source of policy advice on how to improve the status of women. The job was advertised and feminists were encouraged to apply. The successful candidate, Elizabeth Reid, had strong Women's Movement credentials. The government accepted the notion that women's policy, like other areas of policy, needed expertise and specialised advice. In 1975 the Office of Women's Affairs (OWA) was established in the Prime Minister's Department in order to provide bureaucratic backing for this advice function.

At the same time as these laws were being passed, and services were being granted funds, the Whitlam government began to introduce at least limited diversity to government institutions by appointing women to jobs they had never previously held. In 1973 Elizabeth Evatt became the first woman to be appointed a Deputy President of the Arbitration Commission (a body that is now called Fair Work Australia). In the 1970s there was not the same emphasis as today on 'women's leadership', but women were certainly encouraged to move into men-only jobs and occupations, such as elected office. And so began our pre-occupation with 'firsts', with recording and celebrating each time a woman for the first time went into a job or a position that had previously only been held by men. In the 1970s and '80s there were so many such 'firsts' that we often felt we were on a roller-coaster headed for our ultimate and inevitable goal of full equality.

You can get a flavour of this from the following list. In 1976 Elizabeth Evatt became the first chief Judge of the newly established Family Court of Australia, Pat O'Shane became the first Aboriginal barrister and Senator Margaret Guilfoyle, appointed Minister for Social Security in the Fraser government, became the first woman Cabinet minister with portfolio responsibilities. (In 1949 Dame Enid Lyons had become the first woman member of federal Cabinet but she had not been allocated a portfolio.) Deborah Wardley became the first woman commercial pilot in 1979 after winning an anti-discrimination case against Ansett Airlines. Helen Williams became the first woman to head a federal government department in 1985 when she was appointed Secretary of the Department of Education. Mary Gaudron had been appointed the first woman Solicitor-General in New South Wales by the Wran government in 1981, the same year Pat O'Shane became the first woman to head a government department, the New South Wales Department of Aboriginal Affairs. Two years later, in 1983, Susan Ryan became the first Labor Cabinet minister when she was appointed Minister for Education in the

Hawke government; the same year Dame Roma Mitchell, who already had a strong list of 'firsts' to her name – the first woman Queen's Counsel, the first woman judge (Supreme Court of South Australia) – became the first woman Chancellor of a University (Adelaide) and then in 1991 she became the first woman Governor of an Australian state.

1986 was a huge year for breakthroughs for women. Mary Gaudron went on to become the first woman appointed to the High Court that year, although she was not sworn in until 1987. Janine Haines became the first woman to lead an Australian political party when she was elected leader of the Australian Democrats in 1986; Joan Child became the first woman Speaker of the House of Representatives; and Pat O'Shane became the first Aboriginal Magistrate. Di Yerbury was the first woman to be Vice-Chancellor of a University in 1987 when Macquarie University appointed her and in 1988 the first women pilots in the RAAF graduated. In politics, women reached the highest levels: Rosemary Follett became the first woman to head an Australian government in 1989 when she was elected chief minister of the Australian Capital Territory, and was followed a year later by Carmen Lawrence as Premier of Western Australia and Joan Kirner as Premier of Victoria. In 1990 Deidre O'Connor had become the first women to be appointed a Federal Court Judge and President of the Administrative Appeals Tribunal. Janet Holmes à Court became the first woman appointed to the board of the Reserve Bank in 1992. In 1995 Jennie George became the first woman President of the Australian Council of Trade Unions (ACTU), the same year that Wendy Craik became the first woman Director of the National Farmers Federation. A year later, in 1996, Senator Margaret Reid became the first woman President of the Senate, while in 1997 Penny Wensley became the first woman to head a diplomatic mission when she was appointed Australian Ambassador to the United Nations. In 2000 Margaret Jackson was the first woman to chair a major listed company when she was appointed Chairman (sic) of Qantas and the following year Gail Kelly became the first woman CEO of a major ASX-listed company when she took the helm at St. George Bank. And if we went down the ranks in these and other organisations, there were many more barriers being broken and many women moving into jobs previously done only by men.

This might seem like just a boring list of names and, in 2013, it does seem a little quaint to be so struck by women being appointed to such roles. There had, of course, been 'firsts' before, conspicuous and distinguished accomplishments by women. For instance, Nancy Bird Walton in 1934 became the first woman in Australia to obtain a commercial flying licence, and in 1943 Dame Enid Lyons and Senator Dorothy Tangney had been the first women elected to federal parliament. But these examples were quite rare, whereas it seemed that in the 1980s and 1990s so many women were being appointed that we had a palpable sense of not just pride but of progress. Things were changing. There was momentum. There was a sense of excitement at how fast the barriers were being breached, and new precedents were being established. It was just a matter of time, we thought, before it would be totally the norm for women to be everywhere.

How wrong we were.

In November 1975 the Whitlam government was dismissed and, with the election of the government of Malcolm Fraser in December 1975, the Fraser Era (1975–83) began. The major policy initiative of the Fraser years was the introduction of family allowances: a non-means-tested payment for children. This was seen as a welcome reform by the Women's Movement because it was a 'wallet to the purse' initiative: it cashed out a tax rebate for children which had been mostly claimed by fathers and, adding this to the old child endowment payments, created a new allowance that was paid directly to the mother. It was, of course, meant to be spent on children's needs, so did not strictly speaking address the issue of women's financial independence. But it could be seen as slightly reducing a woman's reliance on her husband to hand over the tax rebate proceeds.

It is fair to say that this was a period in which very little was done to advance the equality project. In fact, considerable energy went into simply preserving what was already there. Fraser had the OWA removed from the powerful Prime Minister's Department and relocated to the low-ranking and bureaucratically impotent Department of Home Affairs. Its staff worked valiantly to ensure that existing policies, such as funding for women's services, were not slashed, but they had little influence on the government when it came to new policy.

The National Women's Advisory Council (NWAC) was appointed by Fraser to be his primary source of policy advice on women, thus bypassing OWA. To chair it, he chose Dame Beryl Beaurepaire, a political ally of his from the Victorian branch of the Liberal Party. She turned out to be a savvy and strenuous defender of the equality project, often in ways that never became public. She recruited people like Quentin Bryce, then an academic lawyer at the University of Queensland, and Wendy McCarthy, who was active in the Women's Electoral Lobby and the family planning movement, to NWAC. They were constantly on guard against proposed cuts to funding for women's projects by Fraser's notorious budget review body, known as the 'razor gang', and there were several occasions when Beaurepaire had to get the prime minister on the phone to plead with him to preserve a program.

The Hawke/Keating Era (1983–96) was undoubtedly the most active and effective period since the equality project was launched. The Hawke government restored women's policy to the Prime Minister's Department, renamed OWA the Office of the Status of Women (OSW), upgraded its bureaucratic status, and gave it the power to comment on all Cabinet submissions, meaning departments and other ministers had to treat it seriously. I was fortunate enough to be appointed to head the office in late 1983 and so had an insiders' view, as well as an instigating role, with much of what happened in the first few years of the Hawke government. And there is no doubt that they were exciting times. The primary focus was on women's employment, with the government taking a number of steps to remove barriers to women being employed and to ensure they were treated fairly. The most important of these measures was the *Sex Discrimination Act 1984* which outlawed discrimination on the ground of sex, marital status or pregnancy in employment, education, accommodation and the provision of goods and services, as well as making sexual harassment a grounds for complaint.

There were many positive consequences from this legislation, including requiring the armed forces to open up large numbers of positions to women. There had been a number of exemptions agreed to in order for the Sex Discrimination Act to be passed and one of these allowed the military to discriminate against women if the positions were 'combat' or 'combat-related'. (Other exemptions allowed the insurance and superannuation industries, religious organisations, private clubs, charities and some other bodies to continue to discriminate.) In 1986 the anti-discrimination law was complemented with the Affirmative Action (Equal Employment Opportunity for Women) Act, a law that required employers to review their workforces for their gender composition and to report on the steps they were taking to increase the numbers of women they employed. Later, during the government of Paul Keating and while Quentin Bryce was Sex Discrimination Commissioner, the Act was reviewed and its scope extended, and in the years since there have been further changes, including the removal of many of the exemptions. For instance, the government has removed all restrictions on women serving in the military, including in combat positions. The Hawke government doubled the number of childcare places and introduced various fee-relief measures; the Keating government undertook to meet the entire demand for work-related childcare and to provide a tax rebate to meet the costs of care. The Child Support Agency was established and a system initiated to collect payments from non-custodial parents (given that in most cases the non-custodial parent is the father, this reform was seen as an integral income-support measure for single mothers).

The Hawke/Keating Era also saw a strong focus on putting in place mechanisms that would strengthen the women's policy advice function. This is the seemingly boring back-room stuff that is actually the underpinning of the equality project. OSW, the women's desks that were created in every federal department, the Women's Bureau that monitored all aspects of women's employment, and several other policy advice units generated the policies that were necessary to create the pre-conditions for equality. Just as importantly, they monitored whether the legislation or other measures were having their intended effect. That peculiarly Australian invention the 'femocrat' (feminist bureaucrat) emerged during this period. Many femocrats, myself included, were former activists who now went to work inside government. We were encouraged by sympathetic government policies, by women politicians such as Susan Ryan who was responsible for the Sex Discrimination and Affirmative Action legislation, and by the belief that it was possible to achieve equality for women by working on the inside. This view seemed vindicated when in early 1988 the Hawke government launched the National Agenda for Women.[2] This was a collection of policy objectives, grouped together under the slogan 'A Choice, A Say and A Fair Go', which was designed to achieve equality. They were not only adopted as government policy, and made public for all to see, but they were broken down into targets with timeframes so that progress could be measured. You would be hard-pressed today to find anyone who even remembers we used to have something like this in this country.

A bitter lesson of the past forty years has been the realisation that we have not been able to guarantee that a reform will be permanent. It did not occur to us back then that a hard-won reform could actually be unwound, reversed, repealed. When this occurs, the limitations of having relied so heavily on government become apparent. If a government was not willing to listen to the Women's Movement, what were we to do? We had not amassed a sufficiently powerful external organisation to compel the government to take notice of us. This has probably been our most intractable problem and we saw its full impact during the Howard Era (1996–2007) when we watched women's equality stall and, in many respects, go backwards. As I have outlined in great detail in my book *The End of Equality*,[3] prime minister John Howard used taxation, employment, welfare and other policy quite ruthlessly to achieve his ideological goal of getting mothers to stay out of the workforce. Many of the policy supports that had been designed to encourage women, especially mothers, into the paid workforce were either watered-down or simply abolished. The message was very clear: it was not just that the equality project was no longer a priority; it had actually been repudiated. This came as a shock to many women, myself included. We simply had had no experience of such reversals. Sure, we had read about what happened after World War II when the men came back and took all the jobs that women had done while they were away fighting. We knew that equal pay had been rescinded, and that women were expected to go back home and start on the baby boom. But, we rationalised, that was the war. That was then. Things are different now. Not so, as it turned out.

The Howard years were also exceedingly active, but now the energy was being expended in the direction of undoing previous reforms. Howard downgraded the Office of the Status of Women, reduced the Sex Discrimination Commissioner's powers and budget (and denied complainants access to legal aid), watered-down the powers, and changed the name, of the Affirmative Action Agency to the Equal Opportunity for Women in the Workplace Agency (EOWA). The Howard government was also unashamedly natalist. It wanted women to breed, panicked by the low fertility rate, which had fallen to 1.73 births per woman in 2001. That meant finding ways to either entice, or force, women out of employment and back to the bedroom. In 2004 Treasurer Peter Costello brought in a $3000 cash payment for having a baby and he urged women each to have three kids: 'If you can have children it's a good thing to do – you should have one for the father, one for the mother and one for the country, if you want to fix the ageing demographic'.[4] The Howard government flatly refused to introduce paid maternity leave even though Pru Goward, a political ally of Howard's who had headed OSW and then become Sex Discrimination Commissioner, had advocated and publicly campaigned for this. It drastically reduced funding for childcare, including reducing the amount payable under the childcare rebate. This era of Australian history was all about paying women to have babies, and making it financially less attractive for them to return to paid employment. And it worked.

The landscape of women's equality was drastically altered. Women's choices had been severely circumscribed, especially by the use of financial incentives to steer them back in the direction of traditional roles. The fundamental principles of the equality project, the notion that women should have financial self-sufficiency and control over their fertility, were being seriously challenged, if not completely undermined. The Hawke and Keating governments had not been able to future-proof their reforms. Howard, however, was extremely cunning and he ensured that it would be difficult to measure the damage he had wrought. He abolished the agencies that had tracked and tallied women's progress. He got rid of the women's desks from every department, so there was no longer a person with policy expertise in, say, immigration or foreign affairs or whichever department it was, who was also charged with monitoring the impact on women of policy proposals.

He downgraded OSW and removed it from the policy powerhouse of the Prime Minister's Department to the welfare portfolio. This was a body blow to the equality project. Women's policy was now relegated to the area of government concerned with family payments and safety nets. Even if equality was technically still a policy objective, it no longer had political support. Women had, in effect, been consigned to the kitchen of government. This decision also meant that OSW was no longer able to comment on all Cabinet submissions, advising the Prime Minister whether what was being proposed might have a negative – or even a positive – impact on women. This might sound like a boring bureaucratic technicality and, yes, it was. That was the point.

Every time I walk through an airport in Australia I am reminded of a small but highly significant victory OSW had as a result of this process. My memory of the actual details of the Cabinet submission is hazy but it was at a time when the federal Department of Transport was responsible for the administration of airports (before they were corporatised and, later, privatised). As a result of OSW intervention, the place where parents could go to change their baby's nappies was removed from the women's toilets. This meant fathers travelling with young children could use them and, to underscore this, we ensured they were called Parents' Change Rooms rather than the proposed Mothers' Change Rooms. Sure, it was a small thing, but the equality project is built on a million such tiny changes. In this case, a necessary facility for parents was established which, at the same time, challenged the assumption that only mothers cared for small children.

There was now no mechanism for such interventions to occur in future. The era of the femocrat had ended. This is not to say there are not still many dedicated women within the bureaucracy working for women's advancement, but they are no longer drawn from the Women's Movement. They now tend to be career public servants, whose next job may well be in a totally different policy area. The age of the specialist expert women's policy advisor is behind us.

One of the worst things the Howard government did was to abolish the Women's Bureau. This agency had been established in 1963 by the Menzies government. It was the very first women's policy advice mechanism, existing long before OSW was established, and its function had been to track trends in women's employment and, especially, to advocate for equal pay. The Women's Bureau used to publish reports on various details of women's employment; these were vital tools for measuring a key aspect of the equality project. Its abolition sent a clear, and chilling, message to Australian women: your employment status is no longer of interest to the government. Sub-text: back to the home, girlies. At the same time, the Howard government got rid of the Women's Statistics Unit in the Australian Bureau of Statistics (ABS). It had produced, in collaboration with OSW, a yearly compendium called the *Australian Women's Year Book*. This was an extremely useful digest of statistics of every possible indicator you could think of that helped track how women were doing under the equality project. Now it was gone.

Howard revived the Women's Budget Program (WBP), which had been started by the Hawke government. In its original incarnation it was a brilliant strategic initiative, designed by Sir Geoffrey Yeend, the Secretary of the Department of Prime Minister and Cabinet and the quintessential mandarin. He knew how to make the bureaucracy dance and the WBP, which was an official budget document, released along with all the Treasury budget papers, required departments to report on what they were doing to advance the status of women. (That was the language we used back then to describe the equality project.) The departmental responses were consolidated into a document that analysed the impact on women of the government's annual budget. The WBP quickly gained an international reputation. I was asked to present on it to a meeting of the OECD Working Party on Women in the Economy, and the Canadian government asked me to brief its relevant officials. To this day, governments around the world use variants of the WBP to assess their women's policies and program. But not in Australia.

Sadly, the Keating government got rid of the WBP. It was resuscitated by Howard, but its new incarnation was not the forensic policy advancement tool designed by Yeend. It now became a public relations manual, putting a supposedly positive spin on the policies that were anything but designed to advance women's equality. Today under the Gillard government, that is still its purpose. Somewhere along the way, its name changed. The current one is called simply *Women's Statement 2012 – Achievement and Budget Measures*.[5] It tells us everything the government wants us to know about its policies and programs for women. At least, the focus on equality – now referred to as 'gender equality' – has been restored. If you want to know what the government is doing to advance the equality project, this is the best reference document available, but it's a far cry from what it used to be.

There is now no formal mechanism for pressuring for reform – and monitoring how we are doing. At the same time, there is no single go-to place for comprehensive and historically comparable statistics on women's employment, including conditions and pay. One of the most critical indicators of progress of the equality project has been done away with. As we will see in the next chapter, this has significant ramifications not just for measuring the project, but for the project itself.

With the Howard changes, the context for the equality project was irretrievably changed. Here was a clear example of the misogyny factor. The vision of equality for
women and men laid out by Whitlam had been replaced
by a mundane view of the supremacy of the family where
women were defined by their maternal status and responsibilities. Women, or at least women who were mothers,
were being shunted out of the wider world and back into
the home. They were, in other words, being excluded from
mainstream society, their views not sought and their participation, especially in leadership roles, not required. The
solid legislative and administrative frameworks for equality
created by the Hawke and Keating governments were in
tatters, either repealed or so enfeebled as to be almost incapable of doing the work they had been set up to do. This
meant that the next era would be starting from behind;
future governments would need to decide whether to restore and repair, or to simply accept the new context. Either
way, the equality project had suffered a significant setback.

With the Rudd/Gillard Era (2007 to the present) there
was a clear opportunity for the incoming Labor government
to reset the policy agenda, to try to undo the damage of the
Howard years and to return to the trajectory of progress for
women's equality that had been started by the Whitlam,
Hawke and Keating Labor governments. It seemed at first
that this was happening, although there were a few alarming episodes in the early days of the new era. Early in 2008
prime minister Kevin Rudd announced he was convening

a summit of 1000 of Australia's 'best and brightest' to help map out a strategy for Australia's long-term future.[6] Ten groups were announced that would each have responsibility for an area of policy. There was an outcry when it turned out that only one of these was to be headed by a woman: the actor Cate Blanchett was picked to lead the Arts group. (She was not even able to show up on the day as she was giving birth, so it was arranged for another woman, *Griffith Review* editor Julianne Schultz, to stand in for her.) This incident was one of several that seemed to indicate that women were simply not on the prime minister's radar.

Elsewhere in his government, however, there was better news. The childcare rebate was restored, increased to 50 per cent of capped costs and, initially, indexed. The *Fair Work Act 2009*, the government's new industrial relations law that replaced the much-hated Work Choices Act, in-cluded provisions for gender pay equity. Australia finally became the second-last country in the OECD to introduce a paid parental-leave scheme (the USA still does not have one). The government was clearly and forcefully restoring women's employment as a key policy objective, and setting in place the necessary supports (childcare, paid parental leave) to facilitate it. The government supported, and then agreed to fund, huge pay rises for community sector work-ers, most of whom are women, after a Fair Work ruling granted them equal pay. The Australian Defence Force (ADF) was ordered to open up all positions, which meant virtually all combat roles, to women.

But this was not a total restoration. The Rudd government left the women's policy advice function, now called the Office for Women (OFW), in the welfare portfolio. Inexplicably, Julia Gillard, the Deputy Prime Minister who was also Minister for Employment, for Workplace Relations and for Education, decided to move the Equal Opportunities for Women in the Workplace Agency from her portfolio. It, too, was relegated to the political kitchen. This action was puzzling. Gillard, after all, had a strong background in industrial relations law and in political advising (she'd been chief of staff to the Leader of the Opposition in Victoria before entering parliament), and was a founding member of Emily's List, the ALP organisation dedicated to getting more pro-choice women into parliament. Gillard, of all people, would know how this would look and that it would mean women's clout within the savagely self-interested worlds of industrial relations and employment would be undermined. And that is precisely what happened. Although the government had promised to review and undo the damage done by Howard to EOWA and its legislation, it took a full five years for the new law, the *Workplace Gender Equality Act 2012*, to get through parliament. And even then it fell short.

During the previous five years there had been two sets of formal consultations, run by KPMG on behalf of the government, with employers, trade unions, and, yes, women on how the new legislation should be framed. There had also been less formal and private consultations with two key business groups that had led to a marked watering-down of what was then still draft legislation.[7] (Only intervention by the trade unions and women's groups ensured that the law was not almost totally about getting rid of red tape rather than advancing women's employment.)

Yet after the legislation finally passed the Senate in late November and received Royal Assent on 6 December 2012, the government deemed it necessary to have further consultations on the precise content of the Gender Equality Indicators to be set by the Minister, and which will be what companies are required to report against. These were taking place as I write this. This does not happen with other laws, where the government decides what it wants and, after suitable consultation, enacts it. Why is it that when it comes to a key plank in the equality project, this government – a Labor government, led by a woman – is so timid?

The corporate world is more game. Perhaps realising that encouraging more women into employment is not only good for the economy but essential to continuing growth of our gross domestic product, the ASX established a regime in June 2010 that required listed companies to report on diversity. The ASX amended its corporate governance guidelines to require listed companies to report annually on their diversity policy and on the total numbers of women employed in the organisation, as well as the numbers of female senior executives and board members. Several leading companies became 'early adopters' and submitted their first reports ahead of the formal commencement deadline[8] and, the ASX has reported, there is widespread acceptance by companies of the new requirements.[9]

There is no doubt the corporate world was motivated to adopt these measures to try to pre-empt being compelled to do so by the government. Although there is absolutely no sign that the current government would contemplate the introduction of quotas to improve the representation of women at senior levels in Australian companies, there have been enough rumblings from Canberra to alarm the corporate world. Both Kate Ellis, when she was Minister for the Status of Women, and Shadow Treasurer Joe Hockey have advocated quotas if voluntary measures fail to produce adequate results.[10] The Governor-General Quentin Bryce also lent her weight to the suggestion that quotas might be necessary. I can't see any government doing this although, as I will argue later in this book, I think they should. But I think it is noteworthy that, when confronted with even the remotest chance of compulsion, Australian companies have quickly developed a keen interest in recruiting and promoting women. This ought to be an incredibly hopeful and positive sign. It means that even if governments aren't doing what they used to do, it will be happening anyway. Or will it?

3

Scorecard

You can take your pick when it comes to ways to measure how successful we have been with the equality project. There are plenty of local and international scorings that tell us what we have achieved and where we rank in comparison with other countries. On some issues, such as women's educational attainment, we rank equal number one in the world.[1] On others, women's workforce participation for instance, we are not even in the top forty. We still do not have equal pay, the number of women at senior levels of our companies is still miniscule, abortion is still a crime in at least two Australian states, and domestic violence is a major cause of homelessness for Australian women. Overall, you'd have to say that it is a rather bleak picture. If this were 1983, just a decade into the equality project, we could perhaps feel some pride in what we have accomplished, in how far we have come. But this is 2013. We have been at it for four decades, which is time enough to create a new and equal society. And surely time enough to ensure that the principles that ought to govern this new society are utterly embedded. Yet it hasn't happened.

Earlier, I laid out the two fundamental principles of women's equality: financial self-sufficiency and the ability to control one's fertility. Tragically, it has become necessary to add a third: the need to be free from violence. Alarming numbers of women experience violence, most often at the hands of a partner or other close relative. The 2005 Personal Safety Survey conducted by the Australian Bureau of Statistics revealed that 1,135,000 women, or 15 per cent of all women, had experienced violence at the hands of their previous partner and 16,100 had endured violence from their current partner.[2] These and the other statistics contained in this report are confronting enough, but we get a better, albeit more chilling, picture of the daily reality of domestic violence in this country when we hear the following: 'Victoria Police responds to close to

140 incidents … every day. In every suburb of Melbourne. From Doveton to Toorak – from Hawthorn to Epping. That's close to one every 10 minutes. And these are the ones we know about'.[3]

So said Victorian Police Commissioner Ken Lay delivering a powerful speech on 23 November 2012, White Ribbon Day. He went on to say: 'We often talk about this issue in terms of numbers and statistics so we can better understand the magnitude of the problem. But I sometimes think this takes us away from the reality of seeing women with broken eye sockets, missing teeth, broken arms and broken spirits'. There could be no more eloquent description of a plague of violence that is of such proportions that increasing numbers of companies are now providing up to 20 days' special leave and other entitlements for people who are dealing with domestic violence.[4] This is a welcome and pragmatic response to the lethal danger that many women face from current or former partners, but it is a horrifying acknowledgement of the extent to which such violence is accepted as a 'normal' part of everyday life.

Although around 67 per cent of Australian women are in the workforce, compared with almost 78 per cent of men, almost half of them are in part-time work, giving Australia a participation rate that is 'substantially lower than in many other OECD countries'.[5] For instance, in Canada, 80.2 per cent of women aged 25 to 54 are in full-time work; for Australia the figure is 66.2 per cent.[6] During the years women are having and raising children, their workforce participation rate drops off markedly.[7] The Australian Bureau of Statistics noted in January 2012 that in families where the youngest child was aged 5 years or under, the difference in the participation rates between women and men was 39 per cent. This dropped to 14 per cent when the youngest dependent child was aged 6 to 14. An ongoing longitudinal study of 2000 young people in Victoria being conducted by the University of Melbourne found that in 2009, when those being studied were aged 36, of those who were involved in parenting, only 16 per cent of the women were in full-time employment, compared with 88 per cent of the men.[8] This not only has consequences for individual women who will earn considerably less money over their lifetime than men do, but there are also consequences for the country.

Almost every economist and think tank in the country is in agreement that women's low participation rates are a major inhibitor of economic growth in this country. The Grattan Institute in 2012 argued that if the disincentives to women working were removed, the Australian economy would increase by about $25 billion a year.[9] It identified current childcare and taxation policies as the key disincentives: 'The most important policy change is to alter access to Family Tax Benefit and Childcare Benefit and Rebate so that the second income earner in a family – usually, but not always, a mother – takes home more income after tax, welfare and childcare costs'.[10] Goldman Sachs's chief economist Tim Toohey has estimated that if women's workforce participation were lifted to equal men's there would be a boost to national GDP of at least 13 per cent.[11] The Productivity Commission also estimated in 2006 that increasing the participation rate of women aged 25 to 44 by just 7.1 per cent, bringing it to the same level as a 'like' country, such as Canada, would greatly increase national productivity.[12] Even the federal government agrees, with ministers often citing these and similar studies to argue the benefits to women, and to the national economy, of increasing women's workforce participation. But the government does not follow its own advice: the tax disincentives remain, childcare policy is a mess and women suffer greatly reduced incomes as a result.

One of the greatest examples of inequality between women and men in Australia today is the lifetime-earnings prospects of a young woman who has spent years at university. A report released in October 2012 showed that a 25-year-old woman with post-graduate qualifications would, over her lifetime, earn $2.49 million. The 25-year-old man who had sat beside her in class would, by contrast, accumulate $3.78 million.[13] This report follows an earlier one by the same research group in 2009, which projected that 'if current earning patterns continue, the average 25-year-old male starting work today will earn $2.4 million over the next 40 years, while the average 25-year-old female will earn $1.5 million'.[14] That is a $900,000 difference. That was bad enough, but what enraged me were two further findings. The 2009 report had calculated that 'men who hold a Bachelor degree or higher and have children can expect to earn around $3.3 million over their working life'. Yet a woman with similar education and children can expect to earn $1.8 million. That's nearly half the amount men will take home.[15]

The way I see it, there is at least a million-dollar penalty to being a young woman in Australia today. Not only will a woman earn less than a man with identical or similar educational levels; not only will she earn less than a man with children, but she will also earn less than a man with considerably less educational attainments than she has. The 2012 study found that the 25-year-old woman with a post-graduate degree, earning her $2.49 million for her years of study, would over the course of her working life take home less than a man with just a Year 12 credential. He will earn $2.55 million. Is it any wonder women are giving up and dropping out of the full-time workforce? Is it surprising that only 38 per cent of Australia's Gen X (aged 30 to 45) tertiary-educated women are in full-time employment, compared with 90 per cent of Gen X men?[16] Where is the incentive for women to study and gain qualifications? Education is the one big success story for women. Since the mid-1980s women have been graduating from university at higher rates than men and since 2000 have made up around 60 per cent of all graduates, including in such 'non-traditional' faculties as law and business. Why should women bother to put all those years into learning if they are going to be so penalised financially?

This is, in effect, a gender tax because it applies across all income groups, across all educational levels and across parental status; the only variant is gender. At every level, on every criterion, and in virtually all circumstances women earn less than men.

In the early 1980s when I headed the Office of the Status of Women during the Hawke government I used to travel the country giving speeches about how women were faring. One of the positive trends I liked to identify was the significant increase in women's earnings in relation to men's. Sure, women still earned only 80.1 cents for every dollar men got but, I argued, given the trend in recent years we were speeding towards parity. No question about it. Just fourteen years earlier, in 1970, women earned only 59.1 cents but that had risen to 70.4 cents by 1973 and to 77.4 cents in 1975.[17] In 1979 the figure was 80.6 cents. OK, in 1984 it was down a bit but, I used to confidently assert, this was just a temporary blip. There was no way the gender pay gap was not going to be banished from the Australian economy.

I could never have imagined back then that in 2013 I would be writing that the gender pay gap had scarcely moved in 30 years. Today women earn 82.5 cents for every dollar men earn, making the gender gap 17.5 per cent.[18] But on some indicators it is even worse. A 2012 survey by the business research company IBISWorld of its database of 2000 companies found that women working full-time were getting only 79.5 per cent of average male weekly earnings.[19] The gender pay gap varies by location and by industry. Western Australia, for instance, has the widest gap in the country, with women, on average, earning 25.3 per cent less than men.[20] The financial and insurance services industry is the worst when it comes to women's equality, with a gender pay gap of 32.7 per cent in May 2012.[21] We have to face the grim reality that this pay inequality is still firmly entrenched. You would never know that under Australian law women and men are meant to receive equal pay. As Justice Mary Gaudron, the first woman to sit in the High Court, famously said in 1979: 'Equal pay was "won" in 1969 and again in 1972 and yet again in 1974'. And, she added, 'We still don't have it'. It's now 2013 – almost thirty-five years since she made that observation. And we still don't have it.

Those who don't want to face up to the brutal facts of sex discrimination against women in Australia in 2013 usually argue that these discrepancies can be accounted for by women working at more junior levels, working in lower-paid industries and jobs, by women's interrupted workforce patterns (due to taking time out to have children), and by their greater propensity to work part-time. While each of these factors contributes to pay differentials – although it is difficult to quantify the precise contribution of each factor – this is not the whole story. It's actually only a fairly small part of it. Research by NATSEM in 2009 concluded that 'simply being a woman is the major contributing factor to the gap in Australia, accounting for 60 per cent of the difference between women's and men's earnings'.[22] Women are all too often actually paid less than men even when they are doing exactly the same job. In 2009 the Law Council of Australia revealed that in New South Wales male law graduates were paid $70,300 in 2007 while women received only $63,500.[23]

In December 2012, Graduate Careers Australia (GCA) reported a gender pay gap in graduate starting salaries: men started full-time work 'on a median salary of $55,000 (up from $52,000 in 2011), while females in full-time employment earned $50,000 (no change from $50,000 in 2011)'.[24] These figures were widely reported and caused outrage. Later, in response to the uproar, the GCA tried to downplay its own figures, claiming they had been misread or misinterpreted: that they were based on occupations, such as engineering, which paid more and employed more men. (Precisely!) But GCA also displayed a peculiar reluctance to stand up for the pay equity rights of female graduates, preferring to take the side of employers: 'GCA is entirely supportive of the need for equality in the workplace', it said in a press release issued in response to the publicity around its original statistics, 'and is also concerned that graduate employers are unfairly being painted as discriminating against new recruits in paying one group less than another, which is highly unlikely to be happening'.[25]

In fact it is happening. More enlightened employers are not only admitting there are gender pay gaps in their workforces, they are making them public as a first step towards addressing them. In late 2012 the National Australia Bank (NAB) released the results of a gender pay equity audit that covered about 10 per cent of the bank's workforce and which discovered differences between male and female pay in the same jobs. The difference was a substantial 29 per cent but, the bank said, this was an improvement on the 37 per cent revealed by the previous survey in 2007/08 and better than the industry average of 31 per cent.[26] More large companies are doing gender pay audits and, starting in April 2013, companies employing more than 100 people will be required to report on employee pay by gender under the *Workplace Gender Equality Act 2012*. In coming years, we will finally have actual data by industry, information that will be a vital tool towards trying to redress this blatant inequality.

I am devoting a lot of space to the subject of women's earnings. This is in part because, as I argued in the last chapter, financial self-sufficiency is one of the essential preconditions for equality. But it is also because the gender pay gap is costing us money – not just individuals, but the entire country. NATSEM has estimated that eliminating the gender pay gap would be worth $93 billion, or 8.5 per cent of GDP (in 2009).[27] Misogyny costs us.

The issue of equal pay provokes extraordinary emotions in people, so much so that I think it is emblematic of the misogyny factor. We tend to get pretty agitated anyway by the whole subject of pay – even before we bring gender into it. We tend to see our salaries as a reflection of our worth, not just as an employee, but as a person. We get upset if we think the person sitting across from us at work and doing a similar job gets more than we do. Young women especially are usually surprised to learn that they are not getting equal pay. They simply assumed equality across the board was the norm. When they discover this is not the case, they are often resentful, but rarely are they aggressive about it. Many men are. In the office, they are most likely to express this aggression towards their boss, demanding they get a pay rise. We know that men are far more successful at getting raises than women are. Women are less forceful; they are reluctant to demand an increase in the way men often will. At home, such aggression can turn to violence. When I did focus groups research with women for my book *The End of Equality* in 2002, the women were disturbingly frank about domestic violence in their own lives and in their families. A number of them attributed the rise in violence to the inability of many men to deal with the women in their lives having decent jobs and getting good money. They needed to be top dog. 'I think you need to be very careful,' said one woman, a working mother, from Sydney's western suburbs. 'You don't want to be earning more money than them, you know'.[28]

But I was surprised to find that just *writing* about the gender pay gap can bring out strong emotional reactions in some men. *Why* is it such a hot-button issue? When I wrote an article about the gender pay gap in January 2013,[29] I received a greater than usual number of comments on my website: many of them challenging my use of statistics; others claiming I was exaggerating; a few saying that this lack of equality was just something I better get used to. There's nothing wrong with the pay discrepancy, in other words, some of them stated, as it merely reflected men doing different jobs or working harder. These (all-male) commentators were living, walking, talking expressions of the misogyny factor. That's one way to keep women in their place, was what they were effectively saying. They're worthless, so pay them less. One of the few women who commented had a very different view:

> As a female full-time employee in a legal firm with a typical overproportion of females at junior level and striking lack of women at senior levels, I can tell you that the pay gap exists and is alive and real in my workplace. There are several reasons for this, here are a few good ones off the top of my head:
> 1. Partners need the old boys' network to bring in work. Women don't have access to these networks. They exist and they are real, and you don't become a partner if you can't bring in work.
> 2. Female lawyers at promotion level don't have wives at home organising all other aspects of their lives, allowing them to focus on their careers.
> 3. Men promote men. I see it every 6 months when promotions happen. Women don't go for it because they are not supported and encouraged to apply in

the same way, and people think, oh well, she'll want
to have babies in the next few years anyway …
Rant over. Thanks.

In its gender pay equity audit, NAB found that wom-
en's and men's base pay was the same when they were doing
the same jobs; the differences were 'in the incentives area'.
This goes to women's ability to negotiate pay rises, but
also to the perception of many male managers that women
do not 'need' as much money as men. If you scratch the
surface, some of these managers would argue that women
should not be in the full-time workforce at all. You won't be
surprised that the men who think this tend to have stay-at-
home wives, so they project from their own experience and
inclination. In fact the higher up you go in most organisations, the less likely the men are to have working wives. The
CEOs and the very senior executives usually do not need
the second income the way most households do. It is certainly, as the women who posted her 'rant' above observes,
a lot easier to focus on your career if all your domestic and
childcare responsibilities are taken care of by someone else.
And, would you believe it, there is still prestige attached to
a man whose wife does not 'need' to work. What century
are we living in!

We have no hope of creating a society of equals while
this attitude is still entrenched. It goes to the heart of why
we have fared so badly with the equality project. There re-
mains a deep-seated conviction in this country, on the part

of a great many men and shared by far too many women, that women really have no place in the full-time workforce once they have children. Women who are working are often portrayed as needing – as distinct from wanting – to be employed: her income is needed for the mortgage, for instance. The implication is that if the husband earned more, she could return to her rightful place in the domestic sphere. This is another example of the misogyny factor and it has stalled or stymied our progress in virtually every area of our society. If women are required to absent themselves from the workforce for lengthy periods when they have children, or if they have to work part-time for many years, they are not going to be able to have the kinds of careers that men, or women without children, can have. They will lose the skills, and the confidence, to resume a career path. Therefore there will be fewer women in the pipeline, making it much harder for women to reach senior levels. And this is why so few of them do.

The number of women in the executive ranks of companies that are listed on the Australian Securities Exchange (ASX) is among the lowest in the developed world. In November 2012 the bi-annual census of women in leadership positions in Australian companies was released by the Equal Opportunities for Women in the Workplace Agency (EOWA, whose name was changed by legislation in December 2012 to the Workplace Gender Equality Agency or WGEA). The key result was that women occupied just 9.2 per cent of executive positions in Australia's top 500 companies.[30] Worse, there had been 'a decade of negligible change for females in executive ranks'. Nothing is happening, in other words, and in the view of Chief Executive Women, a conservative group of women business leaders, 'Short of some bold actions, it will be many more decades before the representation of women in leadership comes anywhere close to achieving critical mass, let alone equalling that of men'.[31] In stark contrast to the poor performance of the private sector, women make up 39 per cent of the senior executive of the Australian Public Service,[32] there are four women in federal Cabinet and of the twenty government departments in Canberra, four have women in charge.[33]

In 2010 Elizabeth Broderick, the federal Sex Discrimination Commissioner, established a Male Champions of Change group of business leaders from some of the country's leading companies (which has since been expanded to include the heads of some federal government departments, for instance, the federal Treasury and the Australian Army) who undertook to lead by example in establishing strategies for increasing the number of women in leadership positions in their organisations.[34] It is likely to be some years before any concrete changes can be attributed to these efforts, however there is already some reporting under the ASX Corporate Governance Principles and Recommendations, established in 2010, that require all listed companies to report annually on the gender breakdown of their workforces.[35] The clear intention behind this initiative is to force companies to hire and promote more women. But the CEOs are also going to have to figure out how to future-proof the changes: how to ensure that, unlike as we have seen happens in politics, their hard-won reforms can endure after they have left the top job. This may be the hardest part of all.

Initially, however, companies need to come to grips with the key prerequisite of equality: how to ensure women can 'have it all'. How to ensure that most basic entitlement: how women can be employed while they have young children. As a very first step, companies have to stop firing or demoting women for being pregnant. It's totally against the law, yet it happens all the time. It is often not easy to substantiate since so few cases go to court,[36] just as it is usually impossible to prove that a job restructure that just happened to leave a woman on maternity leave without a position was done deliberately. But the anecdotal evidence of such treatment is very widespread and I am in no doubt that it happens all the time, especially in large companies where it is easier to conceal. The Male Champions of Change need to turn their attention to such practices, as well as to the overarching challenge of how to keep women in their full-time employ once they have children.

Why is it so hard? Why is it so difficult for women with young children to remain economically active? Why is it that in a country such as Canada that is economically and culturally similar to Australia, 80 per cent of women aged 25 to 54 are in full-time work, while in Australia only 66 per cent are?[37] The answer lies partly in Australia's hope-less childcare system. It is difficult to think of another area of policy where the government spends upwards of $5 billion a year on something that is found satisfactory by so few people. Childcare is either unavailable, unaffordable, or insufficiently flexible to meet the needs of large numbers of families. (In truth, it is seen as mainly impacting on women as they are the ones who usually organise the childcare and the cost most often comes from their pay packet.)

In March 2011 the Commonwealth Bank released the results of national research it had conducted on childcare. The headline result was that one in four women are effectively working for nothing.[38] The findings were based on a market research survey of 2000 Australians conducted in November 2010. The key relevant finding was that '31 per cent of families that have returned to work [i.e. the mother has returned to work after childbirth] use paid childcare. Among these parents, 11 per cent say childcare fees outweigh their earnings. For a further 13 per cent, the cost of care means they will only break even.'

It has been noted recently that while government spending on childcare has more than tripled since 2005, the number of children in care has grown by only 20 per cent. In the next four years, spending is projected to grow by 15.3 per cent, but the number of children in care by just 2 per cent.[39] In mid 2012 the government released results of an Australian Institute of Family Studies report revealing that two out of three families with primary schoolchildren where the mother is employed do not use any kind of formal care.[40] The reasons for this are varied but the cost and lack of flexibility of current arrangements are bound to be a contributing factor.

I have been struck by the contrast with France where, according to Emma-Kate Symons, an Australian journalist who reports from Paris, French women have the highest fertility-rate in Europe (2.1 per cent compared with Australia's below replacement rate of 1.8 per cent) and they are more economically active. French feminist Elizabeth Badinter has written a book, *The Conflict*, in which she tries to explain why French women have more children. Says Symons: 'Badinter links it to the fact that they don't have to give everything up: i.e. they go back to work, they don't breastfeed much, they have good state-backed childcare and importantly the culture and the mentality does not heap guilt upon them for doing so. No one thinks it is "bad" to put your young child in a creche/childcare and go back to work. This judgmental attitude that prevails in Australia is almost entirely absent I have noted in France'.[41]

You won't find any 'yummy mummies' in France. Here in Australia, we use that term to describe the mostly young and pretty-much-mainly-middle-class women who have embraced, not just motherhood, but domesticity with an enthusiasm that would astonish their grandmothers. Young mothers today are not confined to the home; they are in the streets, in the parks, at cafes with their huge baby carriages ('Hummers' as some wag has named them) – stylish

advertisements for a choice that the previous generation
pretty much repudiated. Sadly, there seems to be an awful
and growing division between stay-at-home mothers, many
of whom project a self-satisfied superiority at the other
group: the guilt-ridden, self-lacerating, working mothers.
I hear from working women of being made to feel embarrassed because they cannot do tuck-shop duties at school. It
is no longer just a matter of making a choice. Some choices
are increasingly being seen as more desirable than others.
How could it have come to this – and so quickly? Not even
a generation after the Women's Movement fought for the
right for married women to keep their jobs, to have equal
access to promotion, and to be paid the same as men, scores
of women are walking away and saying, We'd rather be
Mummies. And large numbers of them are highly educated. It seems extraordinary that in a country where women
graduate in greater numbers than men (and, you'd think,
would relish the personal fulfilment of having a satisfying
job), in a country where double incomes are needed for
most families simply to make the mortgage payments, that
a minority of affluent women have come to exercise such
influence over the *zeitgeist*. But in reality Australians have
always been censorious and disapproving towards working
mothers. It's one reason our childcare policy is such a mess:
we keep adding to it and patching it up rather than design-
ing from scratch something that might actually meet families' needs. And if it were to be fixed, the benefits would be
almost incalculable. As The Grattan Institute has noted,

'support for childcare has about double the impact of spending on parental leave' in influencing women's workforce participation.[42]

In France, 'their childcare system is overall very professional and well-thought-out and directly linked to the school system (often in the same building or across the road, all very convenient if you have more than one child!),' says Symons. 'Also, there's none of this carry-on about middle-class welfare because, well, welfare is middle-class in France, a country of middle-class people. The state is seen as responsible for providing quality, affordable multiple childcare and early childhood education options for parents. No question.'[43]

By contrast, Australia has done virtually nothing over the past forty years to harmonise not just work and family, but work, family and school. Schoolchildren still get twelve weeks holidays, while their parents get four; the school day starts at around the same time as the office day, but ends much earlier; parents with children in care and in school are required to exercise superhuman logistical exercises, through heavy traffic in many cities, to drop off and collect their offspring, often from more than one location, and before centres close and, in some cities, bundle the uncollected kids (whose parents are stuck in traffic or running late) off to the police station. This is one of the major stresses for working parents, especially mothers who tend to be the ones to do the dropping off and picking up.

One of the most disappointing acts of the Rudd government was the abrupt, and inadequately explained, cancellation in 2008 of 260 new childcare centres meant to be built in school grounds. Earlier, Tanya Plibersek, when she was shadow minister for women, had bragged about Labor's childcare policy in a debate at the National Press Club before the 2007 election:

> You would have heard many, many months ago about our commitment to deliver 260 new childcare centres in areas of high need, particularly on school grounds. That incidentally is the sort of smart policy I think you get when you've got lots of women on your front bench and in your caucus. The people who've actually done the running around dropping the kids off in the morning and picking them up in the afternoon, know the value of ending the double drop off. [44]

It had been a smart policy and cancelling that commitment was nothing short of stupid, especially when study after study tells us that it is childcare that is the essential part of the reforms that are needed for women with children to be able to engage in full-time employment.

The inevitable result of a lifetime of working less and earning less than men is that women have far less superannuation. In 2009–10 they averaged just $40,475 compared with men's average account balance of $71,645.[45] Currently, the average retirement payout for men is $198,000. For women, it is $112,600. As the Women and Super website points out, the Australian superannuation guarantee scheme assumes three things: that you will stay in the workforce for 35 years, that you will work full time for that entire period and that you will earn (at least) Average Weekly Ordinary Time earnings. In a country that expects women to leave the workforce for at least a period of time once they have children, women who are also mothers by definition cannot possibly meet those three criteria. Like so much of Australian society, including most aspects of the workforce, the very structure of superannuation – the supposed guarantee of post-retirement economic self-sufficiency – is loaded against women. Again, the misogyny factor is at work.

Women in Australia today work less, earn less and retire with less than men. This is, quite frankly, a very scary situation. It seems that women are predestined to be economically less well-off than men during their working lives and to be far more likely to spend their final years being financially insecure, if not living in outright poverty. We have institutionalised inequality, and it comes about because of a society and a system where accumulated prejudices and traditions conspire against women – the misogyny factor at work, in other words. And it is this that has blinded us to what has gone wrong with the equality project.

We had thought we were doing well – or, at the very least, that we were making some progress. The notion of progress sat well with our rational, Enlightenment view of society. We had developed the notion of the rights of people to live free from tyranny and exploitation, including the right to the equality of the sexes. And so we measured and counted and tallied our progress. We pointed to increases in girls finishing high school, girls going to university and, before long, graduating in large numbers. We celebrated every 'first'. We cheered when yet another barrier fell and women were able to do things they couldn't have done before, such as become prime minister or umpire a sporting event, and go places where we had not been able to go before, be it the front bar of hotels, the betting ring of the race-course or the bench of the High Court. We tracked the movement of women into the paid workforce, and we tallied up the numbers of women getting into areas, such as parliaments, where they had scarcely been present in the past. Look how far we have come, we boasted to each other. Our mothers and our grandmothers marvelled at how much the world had changed since 'their day'.

We were making progress. No doubt about it. And, we took for granted, that meant we were making headway. We were preoccupied with progress. We did not look at success. We perhaps assumed the two were synonymous. In fact, they are not.

4

Progress v. Success

A lot of people like to cite the fact of Australia currently having a number of women heads of government or heads of state as evidence that sexism and misogyny no longer exist. 'Our Governor-General is a woman, our Governor is a woman, our Premier is a woman and our Prime Minister is a woman,' said Bob Katter, the independent federal parliamentarian from Far North Queensland, in February 2012. He was responding to comments by Senator Bob Brown, then leader of the Australian Greens, that the Prime Minister, Julia Gillard, was being subjected to unreasonable criticism, much of it sexist. 'I don't think sexism is riding high in Australia; if anything it's probably the other way around,' said Katter.[1] Just a few weeks later, following the state elections, Queensland no longer had a woman premier and overnight the state went from having the highest number of women parliamentarians in the country to the lowest (from 36 per cent to 20 per cent).[2] This should be a cautionary tale against using a current situation or statistic as a measure of long-term success.

It is entirely conceivable that by mid-2014 the only female political leader in the entire country will be Katy Gallagher, the Chief Minister of the ACT, Australia's tiniest seat of government. Julia Gillard may not be re-elected in the federal election to be held on 14 September 2013. It would be great, but unrealistic, to expect that a woman will succeed the Governor-General, Quentin Bryce, who retires in March 2014. The Tasmanian state elections must be held by May 2014 at the latest and on current polling Premier Lara Giddings will struggle to be re-elected. A Labor government appointed Penny Wensley, the Governor of Queensland, in July 2008: will the current conservative government of Queensland renew her appointment later this year? My bet would be No. If having all those women leaders was evidence that sexism was a thing of the past, what will we conclude when the country is once again led entirely by men?

I would say that for all the progress we have made, we are not even close to achieving success. I would define success as Australia being a society where women are included in all aspects and at every level of public activity, where women receive equal treatment, and where women are treated with respect. These three things are markers of success: inclusion, equality, respect. And these things are mostly absent in Australia today so that, despite the historic numbers of women in high office, there are still so few of us in leadership roles in so many institutions, we cannot claim to be treated equally when we are there, and we endure an ongoing and humiliating lack of respect. In fact, as I will explain in this and the following chapter, the presence of historic numbers of women in high office has in fact underscored how far we still are from our goal.

In drawing a distinction between progress and success, I am relying on an idea first articulated by Hillary Clinton who, as US Secretary of State in September 2011, made an important speech (that went unreported in this country) laying out what needed to be done for women globally to achieve equality. The speech was to open the Asia-Pacific Economic Cooperation (APEC) Women and the Economy Summit, a gathering she hosted and which attracted, she noted, the largest gathering of foreign diplomats to assemble in San Francisco since the founding of the United Nations in 1945.

Her speech dealt with the urgent need to completely unlock the economic potential of women in order to get the global economy moving again: 'By increasing women's participation in the economy and enhancing their efficiency and productivity', she said, 'we can bring about a dramatic impact on the competitiveness and growth of our economies.'[3] She pointed out that in recent years there had already been a massive increase in women's employment, especially in developed countries, and that this had a significant impact on growth: '*The Economist* points out that the increase in the employment of women in developed countries during the past decade has added more to global growth than China has, and that's a lot,' Clinton said.

> And in the United States, a McKinsey study found that women went from holding 37 per cent of all jobs to nearly 48 per cent over the past 40 years, and that in sheer value terms, these women have punched well above their weight. The productivity gains attributable to this modest increase in women's overall share of the labor market accounts for approximately one-quarter of the current US GDP. That works out to more than three and a half trillion dollars, more than the GDP of Germany and more than half the GDPs of both China and Japan.

So, Clinton concluded, the promise is clear: 'What then is the problem?' And it is here that she made the comment that contains what I believe is a truly revolutionary insight, and one that that should change our thinking about the way we judge how we are faring in our quest for equality. 'If women are already making such contributions to economic growth, why do we need a major realignment in our thinking, our markets, and our policies? Why do we need to issue a declaration from this summit?' asked Hillary Clinton. 'Well,' she said, 'because evidence of progress is not evidence of success...'[4]

Evidence of progress is not evidence of success.

Clinton went on to make the following observation:

> In the United States and in every country in APEC, millions of women are still sidelined, unable to find a meaningful place for themselves in the formal workforce. And some of those who get to enter the workforce are really confined by very clear signals to a lower rung on the job ladder, and there's a web of legal and social restrictions that limit their potential. Or they are confronted with a glass ceiling that keeps them from the most senior positions.

In other words, even when women have progressed into the workforce, supposedly the arena where they will gain economic self-determination and hence control over most other areas of their lives, their ability to succeed is stymied by formal and informal forces that prevent their full participation. I believe these observations by Hillary Clinton are very relevant to the situation in Australia. They provide a useful and enlightening way of looking at how we have fared in the equality project. We have made a great deal of progress, yet success still eludes us. And, although she did not use the term, the misogyny factor, I am going to. When Clinton talks about 'the very clear signals' (the hostile attitudes) and the 'web of legal and social restrictions' (the formal and informal barriers used to exclude women) that impede women's progress, she is in fact describing the misogyny factor.

One obvious limitation to using the notion of progress as a marker is that it assumes continual advancement. It does not give us the tools to deal with setbacks and reversals. So when one or more of our celebrated examples of progress vanishes, how do we respond? I have already projected that a year from now, there are unlikely to be many – if any – women political leaders. We have already had instances of historic achievements evaporating. For instance, in February 2011 a celebrated newspaper photograph of a COAG meeting in Canberra showed the Prime Minister (Julia Gillard) presiding over the meeting; seated next to her were the premiers of New South Wales (Kristina Keneally) and Queensland (Anna Bligh).[5] Tasmania's Lara Giddings was also there, although she was not in this particular shot. You could scarcely think of a more spectacular example of our progress: here were women at the table, at one of the nation's key governing bodies, in virtually equal numbers to the men. But it was a fleeting triumph. Within a year, both Keneally and Bligh had been defeated at elections and were replaced by men.

So yes we had progress – all those women leaders – but have we succeeded in changing the political system so that it is no longer rare, and thus transitory, to have women leaders of our major parties? No, we have not. In fact, the sad truth is that these 'blips' of progress are in many ways quite misleading. They give the illusion of progress when often they are just one-offs, rarely or never to be repeated, rather than signifiers of permanent change. There is a phenomenon in this country where women leaders have been cynically installed as leaders, catapulted straight into the premiership by their parties at times of crisis or dwindling political fortunes. Carmen Lawrence in Western Australia, Joan Kirner in Victoria and Lara Giddings in Tasmania all became premiers of their states in such circumstances. Expected to be 'political housewives', brought in to clean up the (political) mess left by the men.

This does not mean that these moments should not be celebrated and cherished. Regardless of the circumstances of their accession to the leadership, once there, these women make their mark, put their own stamp on the job and become part of history. Having women in these jobs should be savoured, because it is still so rare. There have been only about a dozen women leaders of political parties, at both state and federal levels, in more than a century. There have been some thrilling moments of potent symbolism during the Gillard government. When Queen

Elizabeth visited Canberra in October 2011 she was greeted on the airport tarmac by the Governor-General, the Prime Minister, and the Chief Minister of the ACT – all women. A few weeks later, the same line up of dignitaries met US President Barack Obama when he arrived in Canberra. But more significantly, the achievements of these individual women political leaders need to be acknowledged and honoured. Most of us have no idea how hard it is to do these jobs. It is lonely and difficult, you have no peers, you can't really trust anyone, you get no thanks for your wins, but plenty of abuse from the media and from your colleagues when you are seen to fail. We should be grateful that there are women who, knowing all this, are still willing to step up. It's just that we must not make the mistake of believing that a few instances of progress mean that we have succeeded in creating permanent change. In fact, it may even be the reverse. If a woman is judged to have performed poorly in her job, her whole sex tends to share the blame. You don't hear people saying, Joe Bloggs really screwed up that job, we better not hire any more men. In the case of women, you hear this all the time.

If there were far more women at all levels of Australia's major institutions – in politics, business, the military, the media, academia, the churches, the union movement – then this would not be such an issue. If women were present in greater numbers, they would, in theory at least, be more likely to be contenders for leadership positions in these organisations. They would not be the rarities they are today. They would not be conspicuous for being part of a distinct minority. The occasional elevation to the top position of an individual woman is seen as a triumph for the gender. (Just as a failure is seen as a setback for all women.) In fact it is better seen as a glaring advertisement for the fact that we have failed to really, seriously open up our governing and leadership organisations to women. If we had done so, not only would they be as crowded with women as they are currently with men, but the elevation of women to the top jobs – be it Prime Minister, or CEO or President or Editor-in-Chief or Archbishop or Chief of the Defence Forces – would no longer be remarkable. Gender would not be the issue, individual qualities, qualifications and talent would.

We are not even close to this.

Remembering our three indicators of success – inclusion, equality and respect – let's look at whether the progress we have made can plausibly be judged to indicate success.

∾

Let's start with inclusion. I think it is time we understood that excluding women from any area of society – business, the church, the media, the military, anywhere – is an overt expression of hostility. It is the misogyny factor at work. We have only to look at the gender composition of our leading organisations to see that women remain a distinct minority in most of them, and that in all of them the numbers of women decline the further up the organisation we go.

On the face of it, federal politics might seem to constitute an exception. In January 2013, there was not only a woman Prime Minister and Attorney-General, but women also held the finance, health and community services (which also includes housing, families and Indigenous affairs) portfolios. In early January 2013, the Prime Minister held a press conference to announce the terms of reference and the commissioners for the historic Royal Commission into Institutional Responses to Child Sexual Abuse. Again it was an all-woman affair, with the Prime Minister being flanked by Attorney-General Nicola Roxon, and Jenny Macklin, Minister for Families. The pictures of these events that are beamed out to the population through the media are powerful reinforcements of the notion that women are playing important leadership roles in this country; they tell young girls – and boys – that women can do anything, and so serve as potent incentives for girls to dream big and for boys to see this as normal. It undermines the old stereotypes that represented these positions as being for men only.

But while these images of our women leaders are affirming and inspiring, they tell only part of the story. The numbers keep changing – and not always for the better. While I was writing this, Nicola Roxon resigned as Australia's first female Attorney-General, after only a year in the job, and signalled her intention to retire from parliament at the next election, citing a desire to spend more time with her daughter.[6] At the same time as we are watching women lead, the pool of female politicians is contracting. You would think that federal parliament would be one place where it would be relatively easy to ensure a continuous flow of talent, a pipeline of women to sit alongside the men, and potentially be able to step up to leadership jobs. And it did seem for a few years that this was happening. In 1996 there was a large spike in the number of Liberal Party women elected (from four in the House of Representative to 17), but that momentum has not been maintained and the numbers have slid downwards since. There is depressing evidence that the representation of women in parliaments around the country has peaked and is now trending down again, in some cases quite dramatically. The 2010 federal election saw four fewer women elected to the House of Representatives. The total numbers of women in federal parliament dropped from 68 to 64 (and from 30.1 per cent to 28.3 per cent). In 2013, women make up 24.7 per cent of the House of Representatives and 38.2 per cent of the Senate.[7] This is in most cases better than women's representation in the corporate world, but it still falls far short of equality.

If there is a change of government at the next federal election, we will no longer be seeing the faces of lots of female leaders all over our screens. The coalition's Shadow Cabinet has just two women: Deputy Leader Julie Bishop and Industry Shadow Minister Sophie Mirabella. Tony Abbott made the commitment in early 2013 that his current front-bench team will be his Cabinet if he wins the election, so there seems little chance that this number will increase. If Abbott becomes Prime Minister, his Cabinet will contain 50 per cent fewer women than Gillard's Cabinet (and that is post the resignation of Nicola Roxon). Julie Bishop will not be Deputy Prime Minister. That honour will go to the Leader of the National Party, Warren Truss. Women make up only 20.75 per cent of the Coalition's parliamentary representation, compared with 37.3 per cent for Labor, so they do not have as wide a pool of talent to draw upon. Nor will this improve while the Party staunchly refuses to entertain the idea of gender quotas for parliamentary representation.

At its 1994 national conference the ALP adopted quotas mandating that 35 per cent of all winnable seats must have a female candidate. The result was a surge in female representation. Julia Gillard won pre-selection for her seat as a result of Labor's affirmative-action policies, after having been rebuffed at least twice previously as a result of factional vetoes. From January 2012, the ALP's quota was determined at 40:40:20 to ensure that not less than 40 per cent of Labor Party seats would be held by men, and not less than 40 per cent women. There is now pressure within Labor to increase this to 50:50.

The Liberal Party has always firmly rejected the idea of quotas. 'Every woman on our side of politics has been selected on merit,' Deputy Leader of the Opposition, Julie Bishop, said in an interview with *Mamamia* website in

November 2012.[8] There are 22 women on Bishop's side in federal Parliament,[9] compared with 38 women from the ALP. Is Bishop seriously saying that there are fewer women of merit in the Liberal Party? Or is she just unwilling to acknowledge the blockages that stand in the way of women being preselected for safe or winnable seats for the Liberals? In late 2012, Kay Patterson, former Liberal Senator (and Minister for the Status of Women in the Howard government), was asked to undertake an internal review of the Liberal Party's processes for attracting women MPs. Some within the party were reported to be hoping that she might recommend a rethinking on this controversial issue.[10]

While federal politics might be better at including women than many other areas of our society, it is still a lopsided accomplishment while one of our major political parties simply leaves the representation of women within its ranks to chance and, as a consequence, can only manage a meagre 20 per cent.

There needs to be affirmative action so our institutions and organisations become more inclusive. It does not happen automatically. People have to make it happen. And those people are, for the most part, men. So, in order to have equality, we are reliant on men to make it happen. And if they want to, they can. We saw it happen in 2010 and 2011 when there was a sudden and large increase in the numbers of women appointed to corporate boards. This was spurred on by self-protective instincts, and fear of government-imposed quotas, when it was revealed in

2009 by EOWA that just 8.3 per cent of all ASX 200 directors were women, and that only 5 per cent of appointments that year were women. The next two years saw a flurry of appointments. In 2010, 56 women directors were appointed, constituting 25 per cent of all appointments.[11] The next year was even better: 68 women were appointed, fully 28 per cent of all appointments. It is now not uncommon for some of our largest companies, such as Qantas, Woolworths, ASX and AMP, to have three women directors, although in none of these cases do women make up a majority of directors. Even with three, women still account for only 25 to 30 per cent of the members of those boards. For a short time, in 2011, the board of Pacific Brands actually boasted a majority of women – four out of seven directors.[12] CEO Sue Morphet left the company in August 2012 and relinquished her board position, as did another female director and, in February 2013, the seven-member board contained just two women members.[13] Although in 2012 women accounted for 15.4 per cent of all ASX 200 directors, the highest representation ever (and that's good!), women are still a minority on all boards and the appointments are beginning to taper off. In 2012, only 40 women were appointed, comprising just 23 per cent of all appointments. That little spurt towards equality did not last long. Equality in the board room? Forget about it. The appointments seem to have peaked. And remember that board appointments are easy. Unlike putting people into senior-management jobs, where there is usually a competitive recruitment process, a board chair can pretty much just tap someone on the shoulder.

అ

And so I come to the issue of equality. Too few of the small number of people who run corporate Australia accept that power should actually be shared. Many of them are prepared to give a few women a place at the table, but that is all. They do not believe in inclusion, let alone equality. There is no sign that the comfortable, club-like and masculine culture of these boards is going to be allowed to change. The women who are selected for our leading corporate boards are expected to conform to the culture rather than to challenge it. And while these women are in a minority, there is little chance that they could challenge it – even if they wanted to. This is a great shame, because we would like these women directors, like our female politicians, to be leading the charge in making equality a reality. But, sadly, although there are some honourable exceptions such as Jillian Segal who fought hard to have the ASX corporate governance guidelines introduced, most women directors seemingly have no desire to be in the vanguard of change. Many of them have been chosen because they are deemed to be sufficiently conservative to easily 'fit in' to the existing boardroom culture. Indeed, it is telling that women are more likely than men to have multiple directorships. With ASX 200 companies, 27.5 per cent of women directors hold more than one directorship, compared with just 13.5 per cent of men.[14] In the opinion of EOWA, which reported these findings, 'companies are seeking out proven female directors rather than searching for new female talent'. They want to make 'safe' appointments, in other words. Clearly, they want women who have the necessary skills and talents to justify their appointment, but they also want women who will not 'rock the boat' by challenging the norms and conventions built up over decades by all-male boards. Not that this is very likely. Once they are at the board table, there is little they can do to change the way things are done and still maintain their credibility with their male co-directors – especially if they are the only woman. It can be a little easier when there are two, I am told by women directors, and with three the atmospherics tend to change quite markedly. According to the EOWA 2012 census, there is research that indicates that 'three or more women on the board constitutes a critical mass – the number of women needed to bring significant change to the boardroom and improve corporate governance'.[15] It was also found that 'when there are three women, they are seen as individuals rather than as the "female voice" on the board'.

It can be difficult to be the lone woman on a board. It is not enough simply to be included – important a first step as that is – there also needs to be equal treatment, our second indicator. I have had female directors on leading boards tell me how they have been patronised or ignored – often in equal measures – by their fellow directors. It's as if, one director told me, they are saying: *OK you're here, you've got your prize, now shut up.* Or, the woman director is pointedly only invited to speak on matters, such as diversity, that are perceived as being of special interest to her as a *woman.* The woman is made to feel that the only reason she is there is because she is a woman, that she has been appointed under sufferance and not because of any skills or talents she might possess. Not all board chairs permit such overtly hostile behaviour, but it is notable just how many take for granted that having women board members should not make a difference to the way things operate. So women directors feel it wise to brush up on their sporting knowledge, regardless of their personal interest, so they can join in the conversations about the weekend game that's invariably the small talk before boards get down to business. I have heard a well-known and very senior female executive praised by a male director for her football knowledge. What, we might ask, are women bringing to the table, if they are expected to merely ape what already goes on there? The very point of the supposed value of bringing diversity into a board room – the different lived experience that should produce a different and presumably valuable perspective – is not merely discounted, it is actively spurned. We can only hope that the experience is different on those very few boards that are chaired by women. There are just 6 ASX 200 companies with women at the helm, and only one of these is a Top 10 company: Telstra Corporation, chaired by Catherine Livingstone. The other female board chairs are Elizabeth

Alexander (CSL – ranked 14); Belinda Hutchinson (QBE Insurance Group – 15); Elizabeth Bryan (Caltex Australia – 53); Paula Dwyer (Tabcorp Holdings – 98) and Debra Page (Investa Office Fund – 105).[16]

The misogyny factor is apparent when companies try to keep women out altogether (around one-third of Australia's top 300 listed companies have no women directors at all),[17] or they allow them in on only the most grudging and often blatantly hostile terms. The misogyny factor is in evidence when male directors choose women who will be like them: conformist and conservative. I know of women who were being mentored by leading CEOs for board positions being criticised for bringing supermarket shopping to their mentoring meetings. These meetings are often held at the end of the day, after which the woman has to rush home and make dinner. (A lot of these CEOs have probably never set foot in a supermarket.) Another business leader made a disparaging remark about what he regarded as the over-large handbag his mentee was carrying. If women brought onto boards are expected to behave like men, what is the benefit of their presence? It is the worst of all possible worlds: the company is denied the different perspective women directors might bring to its governance, while the male directors stew in their resentment that they are being 'forced' to recruit women, which means there are fewer positions available for their mates.

If they wanted to, the chairs of Australia's listed companies could have gender equity on their boards within a very short time, since most board positions rotate every three years. But it has not happened – and it won't until business leaders adopt the same methods they use to achieve results in other parts of their businesses. You can call this 'planning' or you can call it 'aspirational targets' – just don't call it 'quotas', since this word seems to act like kryptonite with most businesspeople – but without it, you cannot achieve results. You plan, you do and make, and you measure. This is how business works – except when it comes to appointing women. But rather than admit that the misogyny factor is at work, most chairmen resort to the 'merit' excuse. It's not that we don't want more women, they say, it's just we can't find enough with the right qualifications. The 'merit' argument is an insidious example of the entrenched nature of the misogyny factor across so much of Australian society – in the workforce, in the awarding of honours, in selecting people to run for political office – because it both bolsters the sexual status quo and perpetuates it. It is a view that is so internalised in so many people that you actually have women using it to defend the discrimination that prevents them and their sisters from being included and from being treated equally. The merit excuse is laughable, because it is patently inaccurate. It is absurd to claim in 2013, in a country where women have for the past forty years received even higher levels of education than men that 'merit' is unequally distributed on the basis of gender. It is simply a further indicator of how entrenched sexism and misogyny are in our thinking. We deny women access and advancement using 'merit' as the filter, and then turn around and say they are undeserving because they have not broken through the 'merit' barrier.

So we come full circle. We argue that the presence of women in these top jobs is evidence that our society is not sexist or misogynist, but then we treat these women so badly that they will most likely be demoralised and driven away as well as deterring other women from following in their footsteps. So there will be fewer women in these jobs. Mission accomplished. Not our fault; it's not misogyny, it's simply that women just can't hack it.

You will search long and hard before you find an organisation that is regarded as powerful and prestigious that has a majority of women at its helm. Just look at what are considered to be the most influential government departments in Canberra. Are they Prime Minister's, Treasury and Defence, which are headed by men and have large numbers of male senior staff? Or are they Health and Ageing and similar departments that are run and overwhelmingly staffed by women? You might think that the most prestigious departments would be those that have the most money to spend, but you would be wrong. The Defence Department's budget in 2012/13 is $24 billion,[18] while the total budget for the Department of Health and Ageing is $52.8 billion. Yet the latter is seen as a 'soft' department, with its focus on human issues such as health and wellbeing, while Defence, with its weaponry and mission to kill, is as 'hard' as they come. This perception that a substantial presence of women lowers an organisation's potency and status appears to be a factor in influencing appointments in Australia today. It seems to be akin to what, back in the 1970s, used to be referred to as 'the Russian doctor' syndrome. In the Soviet Union, unlike the West, medicine was a low-status and low-paying profession. This was not because the standards were any lower, or the work needed to train was any less arduous. It was all to do with the fact that a majority of Russian doctors were women. The mere presence of large numbers of women was enough to have an entire profession's standing re-evaluated. So to maintain power and prestige, a profession or an organisation needed to maintain its masculinity – at least at its helm. You might call this 'internalised misogyny', the unspoken fear of allowing women to become ascendant in any of our major institutions, and it seems to be rampant in Canberra.

In 2012 Attorney-General Nicola Roxon had the unique opportunity to make two appointments to the High Court, following the announced retirements of William Gummow and Dyson Haydon. As she remarked on several occasions, many Attorneys do not get the opportunity to make even one such appointment, so she was lucky. There were already three women on the bench, the highest number ever, but now Roxon was being given a chance to make history by making the High Court of Australia the first final appeals court in the developed world (if not the entire world) to have a majority of women judges. There was a list of indisputably qualified female candidates mentioned in media discussions and Roxon herself did not discourage the speculation. When I was writing a profile of her in early 2012, I asked several leading figures in the legal world whether they thought the appointment of another woman would be a problem in itself or a cause for criticism of Roxon. I was assured that, given the calibre of the potential candidates, it would not. In the end, Roxon chose men to replace the departing justices. They each were of impeccable stature and I mean no criticism or disrespect to them when I raise the question: why did Roxon squib this? Why did this ambitious, feminist Attorney-General forgo the opportunity to make history, for herself and for the Court? It would have been a momentous act. The reputation of the High Court is unassailable, one would have thought, so there was no risk in that respect. It was an unprecedented and unlikely-to-be-repeated opportunity to influence the national conversation about what is an acceptable gender balance in our leading institutions. And it was not taken.

A similar opportunity arose in late 2012 when the government needed to fill a vacancy on the board of the Australian Broadcasting Corporation (ABC). There were already four women on the board, so when Michael Lynch's resignation created a vacancy there was an opportunity, at least in theory, to give the eight-member board a majority of women members. The process of appointing these highly coveted board positions is to advertise the vacancies, have head-hunters oversee the process and the Nominations

Panel interview applicants and make recommendations to the Minister. In the end it is a Cabinet appointment on the recommendation of the Minister.

Three candidates were recommended to Senator Stephen Conroy, the Minister for Broadband, Communications and the Digital Economy: two men and one woman. Each was clearly competent, given the selection process, but the woman, with her brilliant television background, was an exceptional candidate.

A man was appointed: Simon Mordant, an eminently respectable corporate advisor and arts philanthropist, but with no experience in broadcasting. Even though Senator Conroy has one of the better track records in the government when it comes to appointing women to boards, he was unable to take the historic step of creating a women-dominated ABC Board. Even with men in the crucial roles of Chairman and Managing Director, this apparently was a bridge too far for the Minister.

Why couldn't these ministers in a supposedly progressive government bring themselves to establish female majorities in these two important institutions? Did they, too, fear that these institutions would be judged to be less authoritative and less prestigious? If so, this is a body blow for Australian women. We are being told, by a Labor government with a woman leader no less, that while it is OK for women to be included, even to be equal, there is no chance we can even come close to running the joint. If Labor wouldn't do it, it is certainly not going to happen under a

Coalition government. And, with this example being set by Canberra, there is no reason on earth for the conservative men who run the corporate world to do so either.

We Australian women now know beyond any doubt what our place is. Not exactly, as a leader of the Black Power movement in the USA famously said back in the 1960s, 'prone', but not fully participating either. Included, sometimes; equal, no. When was the last time you saw a leading businessman greet another businessman with a kiss? How about: Never. Australian men don't kiss each other at business events. Or sporting events. Or political functions. Or anywhere, really. But they do kiss women. It has become the standard greeting, replacing the hand-shake, and almost always instigated by the man. Every time a man and a woman encounter each other in a public situation, the man feels compelled to plant a peck on the woman's cheek – even the Prime Minister's. Why? It is such a widespread convention that it scarcely attracts any comment, but when you think about it, why on earth, in a country as rabidly undemonstrative as Australia, would a kiss be the usual form of greeting between men and women? Would it be to highlight and emphasise the gender difference? Would it be a subtle way of reminding women of their marginal status? Men greeting women dif-ferently from the way they greet each other underscores the inequality. I am sure that most men don't mean their kisses to be instruments of misogyny. They intend them as affectionate gestures, but you have to ask why is such affection now usual conduct in a formal environment, such as a business meeting? Isn't it really putting a woman in her place: among the kissees, the second sex.

※

The third indicator of success is respect. We can describe this as women being accepted as equals and treated with the same deference and courtesy that men display to each other. It means acknowledging a woman's legitimate right to be there, to be included, and to be treated equally. In some workplaces, where men are a majority, being treated equally might entail women being invited to social or other activities they could find rather uncomfortable. For instance, it used to be commonplace in the high-pressure financial services industries for the boys in the office to let off steam at lunchtime or after work by going to 'gentlemen's clubs' where they would relax by watching strippers or lap-dancers. Their female workmates who were invited to join them – they were being treated equally, let's remember – faced an awkward choice. Would they go along and share the benefits, including the often work-beneficial camaraderie, of the occasion – and try to ignore the spectacle of other women humiliating themselves in order to entertain the boys? Or would they decline, risking being called a 'prude' or a 'bad sport', not wanting to be embarrassed by the spectacle – and thereby foregoing a chance for some extra-office socialising that might help them in their job?

That sort of thing is lose–lose for women, but it is also symptomatic of a male-dominated workplace that such activities would even be contemplated. There is evidence that when more women enter a workplace, especially in senior roles, the dominant culture alters and such behaviour either vanishes or is diluted.[19] This applies to supposedly innocent activities such as lunchtime lap-dancing and to the far more serious, sexual harassment, for instance. Sexual harassment is an extreme manifestation of misogyny and it is rampant in our workplaces.

Working without fear: Results of the Sexual Harassment National Telephone Survey, published by the Australian Human Rights Commission (AHRC) in 2012,[20] found that 21 per cent of people in Australia has been sexually harassed since the age of 15, a slight increase since the previous report in 2008 (20%) and that a majority (68%) of those people were harassed in the workplace.[21] Most of these were women. One-third of women had been sexually harassed, compared to fewer than one in ten men, with a quarter of women and one in six men experiencing sexual harassment in the workplace.

There is no clearer signal to a person that they are not welcome in a workplace. Back in the 1970s when women went for the first time into jobs that had been previously only done by men, jobs in the police, the fire brigades, the steelworks and similar traditionally male industries, they were constantly harassed. Often this took the form of photographs of naked women torn from magazines being placed in their lockers (this was long before computers, the Internet and Photoshop gave harassers previously unimaginable creative scope to personalise their artillery of sexual denigration). These days harassment extends to white-collar jobs and increasingly men are victimised too, mostly by other men. And why are men harassed? Is it because they are exhibiting 'female'-like traits? Are they soft-spoken, perceived as weak, not part of the dominant male crowd? So this behaviour is still misogynist, even when directed at other men or perpetrated by women, because it is drawing on the repertoire of conduct designed to marginalise women, to make them feel unwanted in the workplace. In any case, it is women who are overwhelmingly more likely to be victims: they face the greater likelihood of being harassed by their boss or employer,[22] and when they complain about it they are increasingly likely to be victimised or demoted.[23]

But if the civilian workplace is a hazardous place for women when it comes to harassment, the ADF is even more perilous. A specially commissioned AHRC report in 2012 found that in the last five years 25.9 per cent of women and 10.5 per cent of men in the ADF had experienced sexual harassment in an ADF workplace. This compares to prevalence rates in the wider Australian workforce of 25.3 per cent of women and 16.2 per cent of men in the last five years.'[24] Commenting on the report, Elizabeth Broderick, the federal Sex Discrimination Commissioner, said that while the figures were comparable to the broader population, the widespread reluctance of women to report such treatment, as well as 'inadequate or incomplete data collection and analysis' by the ADF, meant the true figure was likely to be higher.[25]

Although it has been more than thirty years since separate women's services were abolished and women integrated into the ADF, and almost as long since the *Sex Discrimination Act 1984* required the ADF to open up to women all jobs that were not combat or combat-related (a restriction that has been progressively narrowed over the years), women are still significantly under-represented in leadership within the ADF. In Navy, of the 52 generalist star-ranked officers, there is only one woman (1.9 per cent), despite women representing 20 per cent of officers in Navy. In Army, of the 71 generalist star-ranked officers, there are currently only four women (5.6 per cent), despite women representing 14.5 per cent of officers in Army. In Air Force, of the 53 generalist star-ranked officers, there is currently only one woman (1.9 per cent), despite women representing 18.9 per cent of officers in Air Force.[26] The military is an overwhelmingly male-dominated organisation that is notorious for giving women a hard time, and its history of sexual harassment and actual sexual assault – especially in the Navy and the Australian Defence Force Academy – is notorious.

The 2011 *ADFA Unacceptable Behaviour Survey*, administered by Defence's Directorate of Strategic Personnel Policy Research (DSPPR), at the request of the Review in June 2011, found that in the previous 12 months:

- 2.1 per cent of women and 0.2 per cent of men
  reported being forced into sex without their
  consent or against their will
- 4.3 per cent of women and 1.9 per cent of men
  reported being treated badly for refusing to have sex
- 6.9 per cent of women and 3.6 per cent of men
  reported being touched in a way that made them
  feel uncomfortable.[27]

In the 12 months prior to the survey, 74.1 per cent of female cadets and 30.3 per cent of male cadets reported experiencing 'unacceptable' gender or sex-related harassment behaviour.[28] I would not argue that the ADF is a microcosm of Australian society, it isn't, but I think you can make a case that it reflects the values and behaviour of the wider community. The pushback against women in the services and their being punished, including sexually, for presuming an entitlement to enter a once all-male domain, are all found in civilian society. The ADF paradigm is something like this: we might be forced to include women in the military, the government might insist that they are treated equally as far as the law goes, but we're damned if anyone can make us respect them. The civilian paradigm is pretty similar; it's just that the behaviour and the attitudes are more widely dispersed throughout society and so are not as easy to pin down.

But what is especially disturbing about the military is that this culture of sexual abuse is so prevalent and so persistent in a command-and-control outfit. This is an organisation that can order its people to kill. Yet it is unwilling (you can't tell me that it is unable) to order them not to sexually attack each other. This sexually predatory behaviour is not merely tolerated, it seems to be tacitly approved since it has been revealed that past perpetrators have gone on to assume leadership positions in the ADF.[29] And the people who think like this and behave in this fashion are drawn from the general society and, once their military careers (usually lasting no more than twenty years) are over, they return to civilian life. There is no misogyny detox on the way out.

So it will probably come as no surprise that some of the worst examples of the lack of respect accorded to the two most senior women in our country were at the hands of the ADF. Each involved separate visits these women made to our troops overseas. The Governor-General Quentin Bryce, and her husband Michael Bryce, visited the Al Minhad air base near Dubai on 4 September 2012 in order to lead the farewell ramp ceremony for five Australians who had been killed in Afghanistan a few days earlier. Perhaps the military brass were miffed by Bryce's surprise visit, or perhaps they were just unthinking, but why on earth would they have scheduled the ramp ceremony for the middle of the day, rather than the cooler early morning or late evening, thus obliging the Governor-General to take a long walk behind the coffins on a tarmac where the temperature 'soared above 53 degrees'.[30]

Six months earlier, the Prime Minister had been treated to another display of discourtesy. Verona Burgess reported in the *Australian Financial Review* in March 2012: 'One of the least respectful images in the past year was of Prime Minister Julia Gillard trying to thank assembled troops in Afghanistan while most appeared to ignore her, their eyes glued to the footy on TV instead'.[31]

It would be disgraceful enough if our Governor-General and our Prime Minister had been treated so disrespectfully in a boardroom or at a university or anywhere else, but this was the military. These are the people who can order a television to be turned off, or a ceremony to be held when the weather is cooler. Is that they chose not to an expression of contempt by the military towards its commander-in-chief and the nation's political leader?

If so, the military is not alone in expressing such disrespect towards a woman leader. On 12 October 2012, the parliament elected Anna Burke as only the second woman speaker of the House of Representatives. On assuming the position, Ms Burke requested that members address her as 'Speaker' rather than 'Madam Speaker'. It's about the position, not the gender of the person who occupies it, she said.[32] She also jokingly noted that being referred to as 'Madam' made her feel as if she were running a brothel.[33] If you ever watch the televised proceedings of federal parliament, especially Question Time, you can't help but be struck by the very different ways in which the Government and the Opposition address the Speaker. Without exception, all

Government members address her as 'Speaker' and, also without exception, all Opposition members, in open defiance of her request, routinely address her as 'Madam Speaker'. It is difficult to recall a greater example of direct disrespect being shown to a woman in a powerful position. It is not just that her request is so blatantly disregarded, but that the federal Opposition, its female members included, cannot resist adding this gender qualifier to the honorific of the federal parliament's lower house's presiding officer. As if to say, *You might be the Speaker, but you are also a woman and we are not for one moment going to let you forget it.* Why would the Opposition do this? Because it does not respect women in high office? What possible alternative explanation could there be for this unashamed refusal to comply with the Speaker's wishes as to how she should be addressed?

Maybe it is merely reflecting the widespread view in our country that women should not lead us. If that is the case, and in the next chapter I will set out the ways in which I believe this to be true, then we are a very long way from achieving success with the equality project.

5

The Prime Minister's Rights at Work

On Monday, 26 November 2012, the Australian Hotels Association held its annual dinner at a posh hotel in Sydney. I wasn't present, but I did read subsequent press reports. During the event our female Prime Minister and our female Finance Minister were the butt

of sexist and homophobic 'jokes' by the so-called come-
dian Vince Sorrenti, who had been engaged to entertain
the mostly male crowd which, apparently, roared with ap-
preciation.[1] If this kind of thing is standard fare at industry
dinners, what does it say about the way the Prime Minister
is regarded by business? Could there be a better example of
the lack of respect accorded to her (and her female ministers) by the men who run the joint?

But it is not just these men at their boozy dinners
who are slagging off at the Prime Minister; it seems she is
fair game for anyone in Australia who objects to our
having a woman in charge. There appear to be large numbers of people, who have at their disposal, thanks to modern
forms of communication, the ability to spread far and wide
their rancid and, in many cases, sexually explicit attacks
on her.

In a speech called 'Her Rights at Work: The political
persecution of Australia's first female prime minister' that I
delivered at the University of Newcastle on 31 August 2012,
I documented in excruciating detail the ways in which Julia
Gillard has been vilified and denigrated by the federal Opposition, by the media and by many ordinary citizens.[2]
When I had been invited at the beginning of the year by
the University to deliver its 2012 Human Rights and Social
Justice Lecture, I decided I would take the opportunity of
this forum to undertake some systematic research into the
question that was troubling many of us. Were the extraordinarily harsh criticisms of Gillard just symptomatic of the

brutal nature of politics in the era of social media? Or was she being singled out for being a woman and in ways that were specific to her sex? I began to research the topic by sending out alerts to friends and on social media (principally Facebook) telling people what I was doing and asking for examples. I had been keeping an informal file of mostly newspaper articles covering some of the awful, and sexist, things said about Gillard, though these were chiefly comments about her hair, her clothes, her single and childless status – the kind of thing that all women in politics (and, indeed, many women in the public eye, especially if they are on television) have to endure. As people sent me material – cartoons, photographs, chain emails, Facebook pages and so on – I realised that I had had no idea just how vile the attacks on Gillard were. There was absolutely no doubt that many of them were sexual in nature, and so would – and could – not have been directed at a man in the same job. There was a tone to many of them that was disturbing and verging on the hysterical. This, I realised, was not just the usual give and take of politics; it could not even be described as unusually robust examples of such cut and thrust. It was something more, and it was something we had not seen before in Australian politics.

In order to try to make sensible use of the material that I was gathering, I decided that I needed a framework that would act not just as an organising principle for the material but as a means of understanding what was happening to our Prime Minister. Since this was meant to be a human rights lecture, I quickly developed the idea of seeing whether the concept of 'employment rights' might be a means of making sense of the material. I consulted the Sex Discrimination Commissioner Elizabeth Broderick and Chris Ronalds SC, who had drafted both the *Sex Discrimination Act 1984* and the *Affirmative Action (Equal Opportunity for Women) Act 1986*. Both agreed that this was a useful way of analysing the treatment of Julia Gillard. Chris Ronalds provided me with specific instances where the Prime Minister might have a case under the Sex Discrimination Act and also under *Fair Work Australia 2009*. In other words, I was assured, it was very possible to make the case that Australia's first female Prime Minister was being subjected to sex discrimination, sexual harassment and bullying.

This behaviour is unlawful and is supposedly not tolerated in Australia's workplaces. What, then, do we make of the fact that it is happening to the most senior woman in our country, the head of our government? I came to the conclusion that these demeaning and offensive attacks are designed to undermine Julia Gillard's authority as Prime Minister. They are an assault on her legitimacy and, because they rely on sexual and other gender-specific attacks for their potency, I have branded this campaign of vilification 'misogynist'.

What follows is drawn from that speech. It has been shortened somewhat, and I have updated a few things. I have not included the vile images; these can be viewed online,[3] although some of the salty quotes from people describing Gillard are still there.

છ

On 24 June 2010 Julia Eileen Gillard became Australia's first female Prime Minister. She had served as Deputy Prime Minister to Kevin Rudd in the Labor government that was elected on 24 November 2007. As Deputy Prime Minister she had enjoyed enormous popularity and initially her elevation was greeted with widespread enthusiasm. Gillard had become Prime Minister by the unanimous vote of her caucus colleagues after she had confronted Rudd and demanded that he stand aside. Although the means by which she assumed the top job were controversial – this was the first time a prime minister had been deposed during his first term – and became more so over the course of time, there was nevertheless a palpable sense of history. This was reflected in the media coverage, with most outlets treating Gillard's ascension as an important event to be taken seriously. (A Tasmanian tabloid devoted its entire front page to a representation of the famous Redhead matchbox made over to look like Gillard.) The public seemed pretty pleased as well. Her popularity rating was high. Women and girls, especially, were thrilled at this milestone having been reached.

Gillard has said that women who were just so happy to see a woman running our country sent her gifts, often jewellery. Gillard said that she always tried to wear these pieces of jewellery at least once, and at an event where she would be photographed, so that the giver could see how much she appreciated the gesture.

Just a few weeks into the job, Gillard called an election, seeking to legitimise her position through the validation of a popular vote. The election, held on 21 August 2010, failed to deliver her an outright majority. However she was able to form a government by negotiating agreements with the Greens and three Independents. In order to secure a deal with the Greens, Gillard agreed to introduce a price on carbon and thereby break a commitment she had made during the campaign that there would be 'no carbon tax under a government that I lead'. Other prime ministers have changed policies or gone back on promises. Keating did not proceed with the L-A-W tax cuts. Howard introduced a GST. Both were accused of backflips and of breaking promises. Neither was called a 'liar' because of their broken promises.

The term 'Juliar' seems to have been coined by broadcaster Alan Jones and quickly adopted by opponents of Gillard. It featured prominently on banners at a rally protesting the carbon tax that took place in Canberra in March 2011. The so-called 'Convoy of No Confidence' rally in Canberra was the first time that many of us were exposed to the virulence of the attacks that were beginning to be made against Gillard. It was the first time we saw her referred to as 'Bob Brown's bitch' and it was the first time we saw a banner bearing the slogan, 'Ditch the Witch'. Little did we know that this was just the beginning.

From that time until at least the end of 2012, Opposition Leader Tony Abbott has relentlessly used Gillard's backflip on the carbon tax to depict her as unreliable, as untrustworthy and as a liar. The notion that the Prime Minister is a 'liar' has now been firmly planted in the public mind. Indeed, the description frequently appears in newspapers without being enclosed in quote marks – suggesting the media endorses this description.

Journalists have commented on Tony Abbott's practice of heckling Julia Gillard across the dispatch box whenever she is speaking in Parliament.[4] Normally he does it *sotto voce* so that only she can hear, but on 20 August 2012 the Deputy Speaker heard him referring to the Prime Minister as a 'liar' and demanded he withdraw. It is 'unparliamentary' to call someone a 'liar'. Abbott's withdrawal was qualified, so much so that he was thrown out of Parliament for an hour, becoming the first Leader of the Opposition to be ejected from the House since the mid-1980s.

This might all be part of the normal cut and thrust of politics. Most observers of Canberra today agree that the current political environment has become especially toxic. The hung parliament, and the Opposition's expectation that it is just one vote on the floor of the House away from government has raised the stakes to levels not previously seen in Australian politics. As a result we are experiencing an era in politics where there is very little civility. The overall temperature of discussion and debate is torrid and people use language towards and about each other that even a few years ago would have been considered totally out of line. This, sadly, is the new norm.

But what is *not* normal is how the Prime Minister is attacked, vilified or demeaned in ways that are specifically related to her sex (or, if you like, her gender). Calling her a 'liar' might not be gender-specific, although as I have pointed out, it was not a term used against back-flipping male prime ministers.

There are countless examples, however, where the Prime Minister is attacked, vilified or demeaned in ways that *do* specifically relate to her sex. Some of the examples are benign, in the sense that they reveal the double-standard of a woman being treated less seriously than a man of similar status. The most obvious and frequent example is the way in which the Prime Minister is often referred to in the media as 'Julia'. For instance, in late August 2010 a banner headline in *The Australian* reporting the Slater & Gordon matter read: 'WHAT JULIA TOLD HER FIRM'.[5]

Have you ever seen a headline 'WHAT JOHN TOLD…' or 'WHAT PAUL TOLD…'? No, you haven't, for the simple reason that previous prime ministers were accorded the basic respect of being referred to by their last names. (It has been pointed out to me that there probably were headlines using just 'Kevin' during the election campaign and subsequent prime ministership of Kevin Rudd. I accept that this may be the case, especially as Rudd campaigned as 'Kevin' – 'My name is Kevin, I'm from Queensland…' – and used 'Kevin '07' as an electioneering slogan in 2007.)

Nor was this an isolated example. *The Australian* newspaper seems to make a habit of disrespecting the Prime Minister in this way. They did it twice on 27 November 2012, with a front-page headline and the banner headline of their A-Plus section.[6]

There is a similar lack of respect in the way the federal Opposition constantly uses just the female pronoun to refer to the Prime Minister. Tony Abbott is a serial offender – often referring to Gillard as 'she' or 'her'(rather than by name) in his press appearances – but he is not the only one.

Federal Hansard shows that the following exchange took place during Question Time in the House of Representatives on 21 August 2012. The Prime Minister was answering a question when the Manager of Opposition Business, Christopher Pyne, interrupted her on a Point of Order:

> *Mr Pyne*: Madam Deputy Speaker, on a point of
> order. She is defying your ruling. You asked her
> to be directly relevant and it was a very specific
> question.
> *The Deputy Speaker*: I actually stated I would listen
> carefully to the Prime Minister's answer as she had
> only just commenced. It is for the chair to determine
> relevancy or not.
> *Mr Albanese*: A point of order, Deputy Speaker:
> under the standing order which requires that people

be referred to according to their titles, 'Prime
Minister' is the title.
The Deputy Speaker: The Leader of the House will
resume his seat. The Prime Minister has the call. [7]

This is politics, you might say. Everyone is fair game.

Perhaps. But should our politicians be the ones to lower
the threshold of what is acceptable commentary about each
other? Sadly too many of them do – in ways that affect
all women MPs as well as the Prime Minister. I was told
by a federal MP that there is what she called 'misogynists'
corner' on the Coalition benches. This is a bunch of members, all of them male, who, she said, 'positively bray' whenever a female frontbencher from the government goes to
the dispatch box to give an answer. And it is not just the
men. Opposition front bencher Sophie Mirabella has been
known to call out, 'Here comes the weather girl' when Kate
Ellis, the young and attractive Minister for Employment
Participation and Early Childhood and Childcare, goes to
answer a question.[8]

Should our politicians be setting higher standards? I
think they should, for the simple fact that it is now possible
to posit that this conduct is having a negative influence on
the national conversation.

I know of people who routinely use terms like 'lying
bitch' when speaking about the Prime Minister. What we
are seeing now has gone way beyond derogatory comments
about her clothes, her accent, her 'arse' (to quote Germaine

Greer during an appearance on the ABC's *QandA* program) and even her earlobes – the comments that many of us found offensive only a year or so ago. The threshold is being progressively lowered, so much so that it is now pretty much in the gutter, if not the sewer.

Here are some other examples, all involving friends of mine, which go to demonstrate how much the contempt for the Prime Minister has leached out of the political domain and into the daily lives of ordinary Australians:

> In Darwin my friend was picked up from her hotel by a cab. The taxi driver said to her, totally out of the blue: 'How could you be staying at the same hotel as the lying cunt'. Apparently Julia Gillard had stayed at the same hotel the week before when she was in Darwin to welcome the Indonesian president. The taxi driver continued: 'Someone should have shot her while she was here. Everyone wants to do it'.

> In Sydney a stallholder in the flower market at Flemington apologised to a friend of mine who was buying some flowers for having to add GST 'for Julia'; he then followed it by saying 'we've got to get rid of the bitch'.

> Another friend told me about an encounter his mother, whom he describes as 'quietly spoken and

conservative-looking', had at a medical office in Albury when she went to submit a form for her latest MRI. The man behind the counter said to her, unprovoked: 'I'll send it off to the red-haired bitch'.

I focussed on depictions and comments about Julia Gillard that are utterly and undeniably sexist. I wanted to establish the extent to which the Prime Minister is being treated unfairly as a woman and because she's a woman. I wanted to identify ways in which Julia Gillard, Australia's first female Prime Minister, is being persecuted both because she is a woman and in ways that would be impossible to apply to a man.

In the course of my Newcastle speech, I presented some visual material to illustrate some of the awful representations of Gillard. Much of the material that is being circulated is not just sexist, it is also highly sexual. The Prime Minister is drawn wearing a strap-on dildo, or her face is photoshopped onto the body of a voluptuous naked woman who is touching herself. She is shown holding signs that invite sexual acts or which supposedly 'shame' her. One that was circulating in January 2013 showed an image of Gillard under a sign advertising the 2011 SlutWalk in Melbourne. She was holding a sign that said: 'I'm proud of the 4 affairs I had with married men who had children. Slut Pride!'

I also presented a video put together by *The Chaser* team on ABC TV's *The Hamster Wheel*[9] from clips of radio shock jocks and their talkback callers commenting on the Prime Minister. Some of these comments are truly shocking and it is well worth watching the video to get an idea of the level of vituperation against Julia Gillard that is being expressed in public by ordinary members of the public. 'She's a meno-pausal monster,' said one caller to Chris Smith on Sydney's Radio 2GB on 14 July 2011. 'Does she go down to the chemist to buy her tampons or does the taxpayer pay for these as well?' asked a caller to Alan Jones, also on 2GB, on 2 February 2011. Another listener called for the guillotine to be brought back – and Alan Jones agreed with her. Ray Hadley, another Sydney shock jock, also on 2GB, described Julia Gillard as 'The vitriolic, bitter, lying, condescending façade of a prime minister'.

If you are anything like me, you probably had no idea that this stuff was out there. Like me, you were probably still outraged by 'Ditch the Witch'. Today that sentiment is tame compared with some of the things being suggested about, or that we should do to, our Prime Minister.

This offensive and inflammatory material is distributed in a number of ways. With today's information technol-ogy anyone can be a publisher and thousands of us are. Mostly we use these tools to benign effect: to chat with friends, to share photographs, to exchange ideas or infor-mation, or just to add a bit of entertainment to our daily lives. But others are increasingly using these same tools to vilify, to degrade and to undermine the authority of the office of the Prime Minister and the present incumbent,

Julia Gillard. Email is one such tool. We are all familiar with chain emails. Usually they are harmless and inoffensive, even if they can be annoying. But sometimes, like the images I have just described, they are downright offensive. The photoshopped image of Gillard's head on a woman's naked body was circulated with the heading: 'I'm STILL not voting Labor'.

I am convinced that this kind of thing has had an impact on Gillard's personal ratings. Although some polls in late 2012 showed the government gaining on the Opposition, even reaching parity on some occasions, Julia Gillard's personal popularity has been either stagnant or falling. Is it any wonder when she is subject to this sort of campaign?

YouTube is another tool. Anyone can make a video and post it on YouTube. What surprises me is that ordinary people would bother to record themselves slagging off at the Prime Minister. For instance, in one such video, posted in June 2012 and called creatively 'Julia Gillard: the world's biggest slut', a young man who does not even have the guts to show his face but hides behind a scarf says, among many other offensive things: 'Hey, just a guess, you also do not like Julia the lying bitch … One has to remember that Julia has the rags on once a month. WHY? Because she deserves it …'.

And Facebook is probably now the weapon *du monde*. In fact I would say that the lethal combination of Photo-Shop and Facebook has taken our political discourse to places we probably did not think possible. I just referred to an example of an ugly PhotoShopped image going round on email. The distribution of similar, or more vile, images on Facebook is much greater because of the massive numbers of people involved.

Facebook now has over 1 billion members worldwide.[10] In Australia, there are 11.7 million Facebook users.[11] So the potential is there to reach significant numbers of people using this social networking tool. Large numbers of people are already using Facebook to express political views. Until I began to do the research for this lecture, I did not appreciate the extent to which Facebook was being used as a vehicle for hate speech. Julia Gillard is not the only target. There is a large amount of racist material and I guess if one were to go looking, there would be many other examples of offensive material. But I was looking for sites that dealt with Julia Gillard and here are a few of the things that I found.

There is a Facebook page called 'Julia Gillard – Worst PM in Australian history'. It was established in July 2011 and describes itself in the following terms: 'This page is a community of people who like to take their anger and frustration out on this useless oxygen thief, Julia Gillard. Our motto is "Friends don't let friends like Julia Gillard"'. This is a busy and much-visited site and it contains a lot of material of a highly suggestive and sexual nature. People using this Page apparently think it amusing to post photographs with suggestive captions, such as 'Sack the Crack' over a photo of Gillard, or a photo of the well-known fast-food restaurant chain Red Rooster, with the 's' deleted. Hilarious. One of the features of this page is the number of comments visitors make about these sexually suggestive pictures. It is not uncommon for there to be five hundred or more comments under a single photo.

And what makes Facebook different from email, or from the hate-filled comments from cyber trolls that appear under online opinion pieces in newspapers or on the ABC, is that Facebook users are much more likely to use their real names and their photographs, so we know who they are. This does not deter people. It is almost as if they are proud of their sexist or misogynist comments.

Facebook has given us new ways to intimidate, bully, harass and defame on a remarkable and previously unimaginable scale. There was another famous Facebook page that has since been taken down. It was part of the Alf Stewart meme – a series of extremely crude Facebook pages that took over the persona of a character in the soapie *Home and Away* and used him to promote some pretty disgusting notions. You will not be surprised to hear that most of these denigrate women and some of them actually glorify rape. The one to which I am referring shows Alf saying: 'Julz, you fucking slut' on top of a photo of Gillard which has superimposed over it the words: 'Smash my box, Alf'. Under that is another photo of Alf, and the words: 'If I wanted a greasy red box, I'd go to KFC, ya slut'. This little graphic had been 'liked' 43,253 times by the time it was taken down. Perhaps just as alarming was the fact that it had been 'shared' by 2,099 people. If each of those people who shared it with their friends had 100 Facebook friends, this image has potentially been distributed to more than 200,000 people.

It must be very hard being Julia Gillard and knowing this stuff is out there.

Does she have any redress? What are the Prime Minister's rights at work? I decided that it was reasonable to ask whether the Prime Minister is being treated in ways that are actually unlawful or even illegal under federal legislation designed to protect the rights of workers. Yet since politicians (and therefore prime ministers) do not generally speaking enjoy these rights, I decided for the sake of my argument to look at the situation in a somewhat different way. I asked my audience in the theatre at the University of Newcastle to imagine that Julia Gillard was the CEO of a very large company, Australia Pty Ltd, and to imagine that they were the company's shareholders. And, I said, let's agree that the people seated in the front row of the theatre were the company's board of directors. I did this to take the audience though the responsibilities and obligations that they, as shareholders and directors, had to the CEO they had employed to run the company.

There are laws passed by the Commonwealth Parliament that set the standard for conduct in the workplace as accepted by the general Australian community. They reflect the norms and expected behaviour within the vast majority of workplaces. One such law is the federal *Sex Discrimination Act 1984*.[12] Section 5 of this Act defines direct sex discrimination as 'less favourable treatment' of a woman compared with a man in the same circumstances.[13] Section 14 of the Act covers the place of employment as the area where such discrimination has occurred. [14]

I think it can easily be concluded that any discrimination against Gillard on the grounds of her sex has occurred in the course of her 'employment' as CEO of Australia. What needs to be established is whether she has been subjected to any form of less favourable treatment relating to her employment due to her sex. I believe that it is possible to clearly make the case that she has been treated less favourably because of her sex. Let me give three examples where she has, in the course of her employment, been subject to comments that are both offensive per se and which relate specifically only to women. In other words, these same things could not and would not have been said of a man.

First, let's recall the comments of Liberal Senator Bill Heffernan in 2007 who said, speaking of Julia Gillard, that 'anyone who chooses to deliberately remain barren ... they've got no idea what life's about'.[15] We do not describe men who do not have children as 'barren'; its usage relates only to women and thus these remarks are a clear example of sex discrimination in employment.

My second example comes from former Leader of the Labor Party, Mark Latham, who said in 2011 on ABC radio:

Choice in Gillard's case is very, very specific. Particularly because she's on the public record saying she made a deliberate choice not to have children to further her parliamentary career.

I think having children is the great loving experience of any lifetime. And by definition you haven't got as much love in your life if you make that particular choice. One would have thought to experience the greatest loving experience in life – having children – you wouldn't particularly make that choice.[16]

I do not think that men are called upon to make choices about paternity in order to pursue careers. This is again a sex-specific situation and an example of a person being disadvantaged in her employment because of her sex. Can we think of any instances where a man has been asked about such choices? Both the original question to Gillard and the use put to it by a so-called commentator constitute less favourable treatment.

My third example comes courtesy of the Leader of the Opposition, Tony Abbott, who in February 2011 demanded that Gillard 'make an honest woman of herself' by taking the carbon tax to an election.[17] The expression of course implies dishonesty and 'make an honest woman of' refers only to women, so is inherently sexist, but, more pertinently, its normal use is in relation to single women. 'To make an honest woman' of someone usually requires a man to marry the woman he has made pregnant. The use of this term in relation to Gillard was a none-too-subtle reminder to voters of the CEO's single status. There could perhaps even be a case here of discrimination on the grounds of marital status under the Sex Discrimination Act.

There are many more examples I could cite, such as:

- the comment made in July 2012 by a Kevin Rudd backer about the time it was taking to bring Gillard down: 'We need her to bleed out', as this person charmingly put it[18]; or

- the recent description by David Farley, CEO of the Australian Agricultural Company, of Julia Gillard as 'an unproductive old cow'[19] – you would not call a man 'a cow'.

But I think I have made my case. No male CEO of Australia has ever been subjected to this kind of treatment.

The Federal Magistrates Court has found that an Aboriginal man who was subjected to constant derogatory comments about his race had been discriminated against on the grounds of race.[20] I suggest that were such a case to be brought forward based on what Julia Gillard has had to endure there would be a finding of sex discrimination. This then creates obligations for the board of directors of Australia Pty Ltd, I argued, to rectify the situation and remove the discrimination or else risk being held liable for the damage done to her – both to her reputation and to her emotional wellbeing.

I think we can also make the case that the CEO has been subject to sexual harassment in her employment as set out by sections 28A and 28B of the Sex Discrimination Act.[21]

It is well accepted under the Act that the sending of sexually explicit material via email or text to a person constitutes sexual harassment.[22] The definition also covers accessing sexually explicit Internet sites. The creating of sexually explicit Internet sites or contributing to ones on Facebook that I have described would easily fall within the definition of sexual harassment. (What has not yet been tested in court is whether being exposed to pornography at work constitutes discrimination. A case involving an air-traffic controller whose manager regularly emailed pornography to colleagues who viewed it in her presence, and who was sacked for instigating the court action, was settled out of court in August 2012.[23])

One person who has made an artform out of creating sexually explicit images of the Prime Minister is Larry Pickering. He became infamous after being identified by Gillard in her press conference on Thursday, 23 August 2012, as someone who publishes 'a vile and sexist website'. Gillard said: 'for many, many months now I have been the subject of a very sexist smear campaign from people for whom I have no respect'. What she did not say is that for many months Pickering had bombarded, not just her, but every member of federal parliament and every senator on almost a daily basis with emails containing hate-filled commentary about Gillard. Often these commentaries were accompanied by loathsome cartoons, many of which depict Gillard naked and wearing a huge strap-on dildo. Pickering was notorious back in the days when he was cartoonist for *The Australian* for producing annual calendars in which the then all-male politicians had extremely long penises that were used to supposedly entertaining effect. It seems that Pickering cannot envisage a Prime Minister without a penis – so he had to give Gillard a strap-on. When Facebook (where he now publishes his material), forced him to stop drawing her with a strap-on, he started depicting her with a long brown, seemingly leather, dildo thrown over her shoulder.[24]

I saw many examples of these emails – shown to me by MPs – and I was aware (1) that they go to every member and senator, and (2) they contain vile and disgusting images of our political leaders (most often Julia Gillard and, until his resignation from Parliament, Leader of the Greens, Bob Brown). Yet no Member of Parliament denounced them, not in public at least. I found this almost beyond comprehension. Nor, before Gillard mentioned them at her press conference, had they been written about by anyone in the parliamentary press gallery. Surely it was newsworthy that Australia's first female Prime Minister was under such constant illustrated attack. Surely it was noteworthy that the portrayals of her are obscene and indisputably sexist.

Surely it would have merited a report somewhere in the media by one of the journalists who churn out stories daily from Canberra. Instead we had what one might almost call a conspiracy of silence.

Is it because the images are so vile that there was an implicit agreement between parliamentarians and the press to simply pretend they did not exist? Or were they just dismissed as the work of a cranky old hack? I sense that many journalists in the press gallery are now somewhat embarrassed about their failure to report on and thereby smoke out these endless vicious attacks on the Prime Minister.

And there is now the conundrum about how to deal with the fact that Pickering is still producing these vile cartoons. If anything, the publicity has emboldened him and urged him to even lower depths. On 23 January 2013 he produced, on his Facebook page, a particularly obnoxious response to the announcement by Gillard that she had exercised what she called a 'captain's pick' to intervene in a pre-selection in the Northern Territory. Gillard had asked the sitting member, Senator Trish Crossin, to stand aside in favour of a new recruit, the Aboriginal Olympic gold medalist Nova Peris. Crossin made no secret of the fact that she was extremely unhappy about being shoved out of her seat like this. Pickering drew a cartoon entitled 'Secret Women's Business' that showed a prostrate, but fully dressed, Crossin lying on the red earth, her backside pointing up, with a naked Gillard pointing a large brown dildo at her posterior. Standing beside Gillard was a representation of Peris, also naked and looking embarrassed. Gillard has a bubble coming out of her mouth saying 'Old Welsh custom called pointing the boner'. This cartoon was shared 497 times, 'liked' by 839 people and, by 25 January, had attracted 342 comments. One of these, interestingly enough, was from Pickering himself.[25] He said, in response to a comment by someone else that 'Facebookwill ban me if I draw nipples [on the Prime Minister]. It seems ok on indigenous birds tho'. He had drawn nipples on Peris, but not on Gillard.

My comment is this: why does Facebook deem it OK for a cartoonist to continually represent the Prime Minister wielding a huge dildo (and often using it to seemingly attack people), but draws the line at having her portrayed with nipples? Something is very wrong here.

Social media allows everyone to express themselves to large audiences in ways that were inconceivable before the Internet. Unfortunately some people abuse this freedom of expression to abuse and bully others, often using sexual language and images to do so. Women with a strong online presence are especially vulnerable to such attacks. It is quite astonishing the things people are prepared to say on Facebook and Twitter, and in emails, often using their real names. Not only do they appear to have no inhibitions or any shame, they often exhibit strong misogynist tendencies. This so-called 'e-bile' that is specifically anti-women has been documented by academic Emma Jane in a paper called 'Your a Ugly, Whorish, Slut' [sic].[26] Many of us who are frequent users of social media are only too familiar with this kind of abuse. What shocked many of us was that the Prime Minister was on the receiving end of it as well.

Returning to the Prime Minister's rights at work, it is possible to make the case that the CEO of Australia Pty Ltd has been bullied. Comcare, the Commonwealth workplace health and safety agency, defines bullying as: 'Repeated behaviour that could reasonably be considered to be humiliating, intimidating, threatening or demeaning to a person, or group of persons, and which therefore creates a risk to health and safety'.[27] There can be little doubt that these sexually explicit images of Julia Gillard by her abusive detractors are acts of bullying, in the sense that they are solely designed to demean and diminish her, humiliate and intimidate her.

Turning to industrial relations law, would the CEO have any resort under the *Fair Work Act 2009 (Cth)*? Section 340 prohibits an employer from taking 'adverse action' against an employee, which includes discriminating against an employee. Section 351 prohibits an employer from taking adverse action against an employee because of the employee's sex or marital status. An employer can be liable for the actions of their employees and for the way co-workers treat each other. Increasingly, industrial tribunals and commissions are being called upon to determine whether conduct on Facebook can warrant dismissal.

Already there are many examples where Fair Work Australia has been cited when employees have been dismissed for acts of sexual harassment or inappropriate conduct on social media sites, such as Facebook, against co-workers. (This definition includes supervisors and bosses, as well as more junior employees.)[28] While the tests may be different from those under sex discrimination law, there is little doubt that the type of commentary and images to which Julia Gillard is routinely and repeatedly subjected would come within the type of conduct prohibited in all other workplaces. An employer would be liable to their employee and might have to pay a civil penalty (a fine) under section 539. (Indeed, there could even be the possibility of prison. In July a Bendigo magistrate gave a suspended prison sentence to the creator of the Facebook page, 'Benders Root-Rate'. Yes, that does mean what you think it means: a Facebook page in which the creators rated named people's sexual performance.)

Aren't we now witnessing a similar process to what happened in the 1970s when women went for the first time into previously male-dominated jobs and were harassed with pornographic photographs placed inside their lockers? When Julia Gillard logs onto her computer and sees images of herself naked, or holding suggestive signs, isn't she being subjected to similarly hostile acts by people who apparently resent her being in the job? I would say 'Yes'.

So my speech argued that it was fair to conclude that the CEO of Australia Pty Ltd has been subject to conduct that is outlawed under both the Sex Discrimination Act and the Fair Work Act. I suggested to the audience that they, as shareholders of Australia Pty Ltd, would expect the board of directors of the company to not just pay any applicable fines and damages, but to do something about changing the culture of the company that allows this kind of behaviour to flourish. The courts can make orders to stop certain conduct and can order other conduct to occur; shareholders can also demand the directors put in place some positive actions. In saying this to the audience, I was trying to make the larger point that all of us, all we Australians, are in effect shareholders in the company that has hired Julia Gillard and that all of us can (and should) demand that this conduct stop. It is we who will have to take responsibility for changing the culture of our country. As I will demonstrate later, there have been some positive steps in this respect.

I hoped that in making the case in the way that I did – using laws governing workplace conduct to illustrate how unfairly the Prime Minister has been treated *as an employee* – that I was persuasive in making the case that the Prime Minister is entitled to feel aggrieved by the way she is being treated.

But, I also argued, so are we. It says something about our country and about us that we could subject our leader to such vile abuse. It is even worse that we somehow think it is OK and even funny to demean her sexually in such crude and disgusting ways. What has happened to us? How can we account for these levels of vitriol, for this hatred? Can it really be the case that *a tax* – a carbon tax – could really spur so many people to such levels of hatred? I find that impossible to believe, so I have had to conclude that the persecution of Julia Gillard has to be about something else. Is it just the simple fact that she is a woman?

It is difficult not to conclude that we Australians are – so far at least – simply incapable of accepting a woman being in charge of our country. It is worth remembering that we were one of the last countries in our region to have a female Prime Minister or President. India, Sri Lanka, Pakistan, the Philippines, Bangladesh, South Korea and, of course, New Zealand – who managed two! – all had women leaders before we did. But surely Julia Gillard's continuing unpopularity is not just because she is a woman? It can't be because, remember, she was incredibly popular as Deputy Prime Minister.

There are two reasons why Australians are having difficulty liking their Prime Minister. For all of our history a prime minister has been a man in a suit who has been married (to a woman) and who has children. If our first female leader also happens to be our first unmarried, living with a partner, childless, not to mention atheist, Prime Minister, then perhaps it is not surprising that the population is having some trouble getting their heads around this new reality. The fact that we have had ten female leaders at state or territory level apparently has not adequately prepared us for this.

But I think there is something else at work. And that is the deliberate sabotaging of the Prime Minister by political enemies, who include people within her own party, who are using an array of weapons that include personal denigration, some of it of a sexual or gendered nature, to undermine her and erode her authority.

It was not always so.

I like to quote a story that did the rounds in Sydney a couple of years ago about the hard men of the New South Wales Right who got very nervous when they learned that then Deputy Prime Minister Julia Gillard was planning to attend a big Labor function in the western suburbs. How would the traditional women of the west react to Gillard, the Sussex Street boys fretted: after all, she was single, had no kids and lived with a hairdresser. They made some inquiries and the feedback shocked them: these supposedly traditional women had no problems with Gillard's marital status, envied her freedom from the responsibilities of raising children and, most of all, were in awe of her for choosing a hairdresser for a partner![29]

In June 2010, in the week she became Prime Minister, Gillard presided over a 14 per cent increase in her party's vote, with Labor's two-party preferred vote rising to 55 per cent versus the Coalition's 45 per cent. Julia Gillard was preferred as Prime Minister by 55 per cent of Australians against the 34 per cent who preferred Tony Abbott.[30] Even more striking, as ABC journalist Barrie Cassidy has pointed out, was the stunning turnaround in the leader's satisfaction rating. Kevin Rudd's rating when he was deposed had been −19. Within a week of becoming Prime Minister, Julia Gillard's satisfaction rating was +19, a 38 points turnaround.[31] It is difficult to remember back three years ago to Julia Gillard's rock-star status. She was popular, even adored, and there was no doubt she was on track to lead Labor to a stunning electoral victory. And then there were the leaks.

During the election campaign several extremely damaging leaks, put into the public domain by journalist Laurie Oakes, alleged that in Cabinet before the leadership change Gillard had opposed both the paid parental-leave scheme and increases to the aged pension. Nothing could have been more calculated to wound her politically. She – the childless woman – stood accused of not caring about families with children (paid parental leave) and of being a heartless person who was against fairness for pensioners. Gillard's popularity dropped almost 20 points virtually overnight following the leak on 27 July 2010 about her supposedly not supporting the paid parental-leave scheme, and – as we all know – the government's standing was damaged, its primary vote fell to 38 per cent[32] and it was unable to gain a parliamentary majority in order to govern.

Gillard has never recovered from this.

Her personal popularity remained low even while the government's standing started to improve towards the end of 2012. And she never will recover while a similarly brutal and targeted campaign of vilification is being conducted against her. In 2010, those cruelly targeted leaks successfully struck at her credibility and her authority. According to journalist Barrie Cassidy, 'Whatever the motivation behind the story, it left few people in the Labor Party in any doubt that the source was either Kevin Rudd or someone acting on his behalf, with or without his consent'.[33] In 2013, in addition to the continuing attacks on her by the Rudd camp (where Gillard is routinely referred to as a 'bitch' by some of her parliamentary colleagues), she struggles under the burden of anyone who forwards a viral email, or 'likes' or 'shares' or adds to a sexist comment on Facebook, who reTweets a crude comment, or engages in casual conversations where she, the country's leader, is dismissed as a 'lying bitch'.

My purpose in deciding to explore these things in the Newcastle speech, and in making them available subsequently on my website, was not to titillate, and it was certainly not to give satisfaction to the people who were responsible for producing this awful material. In fact, some people counselled me not to show it. Ignore it, delete it, don't reinforce it, I was told. I disagreed.

I felt then, and I still feel, that by shining a light on what is out there – on the ways in which our country's leader is being demeaned and destabilised, and our country and its population is degrading itself – we might be able to shame the more decent among us into not going along with it any more. We have to do this, I argued then and I feel even more strongly now, because I am alarmed that we have created a climate of misogyny that is widespread and contagious. It taints all of us, makes all women vulnerable and it is likely to act as a deterrent to young women thinking about a career in politics. Why would anyone want to step up for such treatment?

So, I concluded, we need to take some action: to draw a line; to be the ones to say that we have had enough. I was very impressed when Helen Szoke, at the time the Race Discrimination Commissioner, in mid August 2012 unveiled a strategy to end racism in this country: 'Racism: it stops with me'. Simple, yet effective. I argued that we citizens, we shareholders in Australia Pty Ltd, should make a similar commitment: 'The persecution of our Prime Minister: it stops with me'.

So, I said, next time you get one of those emails, don't delete it – send it back to whomever sent it to you and tell them: It stops with me. When someone in your company refers to the Prime Minister disrespectfully, don't ignore it – tell them off: it stops with me. And if you stumble across a website or a Facebook page that contains offensive commentary or images, don't avert your eyes – make a comment calmly saying how sad this makes you feel: it stops with me.

This is something that is beyond party, beyond political affiliation, beyond voting intention and beyond whether or not you like Julia Gillard. We should all be worried about this vilification of our first female Prime Minister. I think the same thing would happen if she were from the Liberal Party. Indeed Julie Bishop, the Deputy Leader of the Opposition has told me that she is constantly attacked for being childless. So it does not matter whether you are

Labor or Liberal, National Party or Green, whether you admire Julia Gillard or you despise her, whether you intend to vote for her or against her. If enough of us push back, perhaps we can stop it. And if we can, perhaps that will help restore some dignity and respect to the holder of our highest office – and to women generally. Australia would be a better place if we could.

Even though not all of us were guilty of the conduct that I have documented, all of us bear some responsibility for it being tolerated and continued. I would like to think that my Newcastle speech will stand as a record of a moment in our history, a documenting of when we as a country failed in our duty as citizens to treat our leader with civility and respect. I also hope that it may have served as a wake-up call and thus prompted us to behave differently.

In the next chapter, I will describe some of the reactions that have heartened and encouraged me to believe that we are capable of rising above all this.

6

Destroying the Joint

As I was driving up to Newcastle on 31 August 2012 to deliver my speech, reports began to come through that Sydney broadcaster Alan Jones had that morning attacked several high-profile women leaders as he addressed a small rally outside Sydney Town Hall. Later I learned that he had denounced Prime Minister Julia Gillard for having announced the previous day, while she was attending a Pacific Islands Forum meeting in the Cook Islands, that Australia would provide $320 million, over ten years, for programs designed to reduce violence against women in the Pacific.[1] Jones's attack also included former Victorian police commissioner Christine Nixon and Sydney Lord Mayor Clover Moore as examples of women who, he said, were 'destroying the joint'. Normally the rantings of Alan Jones would merely be reinforcing fodder to the prejudices of his dwindling and ageing radio audience, but this time they sparked a flame in the broader community. That evening, the writer and commentator Jane Caro took to Twitter with a wry comment:

> Got time on my hands this Friday night so am
> sitting around coming up with ways to destroy the
> joint, being a woman and all. Ideas welcome.

The hashtag #destroyingthejoint was created that night. It started off as a bit of fun, but with others soon jumping onto Twitter with their own semi-serious suggestions about how to destroy the joint, it quickly developed momentum. 'The hashtag trended worldwide and a Facebook page, merchandise and more sprang into being,' Jane Caro wrote a few months later in an article that described the way in which women were galvanised into action in 2012. 'For the first time, women didn't have to cop insults about their gender in impotent silence. Thanks to social media and the unmediated (by men) access it gave them to the public conversation they could – and did – make their point of view heard and heard loudly'.[2]

Jones's intended insult, that women were 'destroying the joint', was turned on its head. It wasn't the first time that women had transformed what was intended to be a belittling comment into a triumphant battle cry. In 1905 the *Daily Mail* newspaper in Britain ridiculed the suffragists – those, mostly women, who were fighting to get the vote for women, by calling them 'suffragettes'.[3] The more radical of the suffragists embraced the term. They started using it with pride to describe themselves, and to differentiate themselves as radicals from those who used more moderate tactics. They created a publication, *The Suffragette*. More than a century later in another country, Australian women also took the disparagement and created the modern-day equivalent of a campaign newspaper, the Facebook[4] page and the Twitter handle @JointDestroyer. Yes, that's right, women responded. We are going to destroy the joint. We utterly reject a joint whose sexism and misogyny is so ingrained that far too many people see it as perfectly normal behaviour. We will no longer tolerate a joint that systematically excludes women from its ranks, that insults us as a matter of course when we stand up for ourselves, a joint that sees something wrong with spending money to stop violence against women. If that's what the joint is, we don't want it. It is noteworthy that 2GB, the radio station that employs Alan Jones, does not have a single woman presenter. Not one. In 2013.

It soon became obvious that there was a lot of pent-up anger and frustration simmering just below the surface with large numbers of Australian women. The formal Women's Movement might be in abeyance, 'feminism' might be a dirty word with a lot of women and it might have seemed that the passion and activism that marked the 1970s were long gone – but then a number of things happened that ignited passions and activism that turned out not to be gone after all. The second half of 2012 saw an eruption of rage by women of all ages about the way Australia's first female Prime Minister was being treated. My Newcastle speech had an unexpectedly large response as thousands went to my website to read it and it was widely shared across social media. Many people welcomed what was described by Jane Caro as a 'forensic analysis of the gendered abuse being thrown at Gillard...'.[5] I was asked to present the speech on two subsequent occasions, and it was reprinted in a number of publications, including two scholarly journals published by universities. But my speech would not have had anything like the same impact had Gillard herself not drawn attention to the 'misogynists and the nut jobs on the Internet' at a press conference just a week earlier, on 23 August 2012.[6] Nor would its documentation of Gillard's persecution have struck such a chord had Alan Jones not, a few weeks later, made a horrifying comment about Gillard's father at what he thought was a private function, but which a reporter tape-recorded. On Saturday, 22 September 2012, Jones was the guest speaker at a University of Sydney Liberal Club dinner held at the Watermark restaurant at Circular Quay: 'The old man recently died a few weeks ago of shame,' Jones told the audience, that included several federal party MPs. 'To think that he had a daughter who told lies every time she stood for parliament. Every person in the caucus of the Labor Party knows that Julia Gillard is a liar.'[7]

Jones issued an apology once his remarks were made public, yet this did nothing to stop revulsion being widely expressed at what he had said. Gillard's much-loved father had died suddenly just weeks earlier, while she was attending an APEC meeting in Russia. It then emerged that Jones had made the comments while wearing a jacket made of a chaff bag, which he had signed and won at a raffle held at the dinner. The jacket referred to a remark he had made on his radio program on 6 July 2011 about Gillard: 'The woman is off her tree and quite frankly they should shove her and Bob Brown in a chaff bag and take them as far out to sea as they can and tell them to swim home'.[8] Jones had subsequently said he regretted these remarks (which had also caused a storm of outrage), but his willingness to wear a chaff bag as a garment at the Liberal dinner suggested his regrets were insincere, if not downright confected.

'Destroy the joint' was almost overnight transformed into a full-scale political campaign with the dedicated goal of getting advertisers to desert Jones's program. An online petition organised by the group change.org also put on the pressure and quickly gathered more than 100,000 signatures. The whole exercise was a stunning success.

Well-known brands such as Telstra, Coles, Woolworths and Medibank suspended advertising on Jones's program and some companies pulled their ads from the entire station. Mercedes Benz took back the expensive car it had given Jones. Within a week, the withdrawing of advertising had become so widespread – and no doubt so expensive to the station – that drastic action was called for. On 7 October 2012, Russell Tate, the executive chairman of the Macquarie Radio Network, owners of 2GB, announced that all advertising on Jones's program would be suspended. This was clearly a pre-emptive strike to stop the damaging daily stories about more and more advertisers deserting the show.[9] Tate also made an attempt to portray Jones and the station as the victims, claiming they and their advertisers had been subjected to 'cyber-bullying'. The official suspension lasted for more than a week[10] and it was never clear how many of Jones's former advertisers returned or whether some of them had now reached the view, like many other Australians, that Alan Jones's abusive and offensive style of showmanship was no longer tolerable. It looked like he was finished. With his highly personal and misogynist attacks on the Prime Minister, he had simply gone too far. Way too far.

The 'Destroy the joint' campaign was a specific response to a specific set of comments by Jones, but it represented far more than that. Part of the reason for its success was that it had become something of a lightning rod. It was the last straw. It was the line in the sand. It was the bridge too far. The point of no return. It was all of those things. A point had been reached when enough women had had enough of being insulted, of being excluded, of being told, in effect: 'This is our country, girlie, our joint, not yours. We make the rules; we decide who gets to run the show; we decide what's a fair thing. Not you. You are destroying the joint'. And women responded, in huge numbers, with the affirmation: 'Yep, that's right. We are. And if we weren't before, we certainly are now. We have had enough of that old sexist, misogynist joint that does not want us around, that treats us so poorly, that demeans us and shames us, that tells us how we are supposed to behave in our country'.

Just two days after the Joint Destroyers had forced Jones's program to go advertiser-free, the Prime Minister rose in the House of Representatives one afternoon and delivered the speech that would define her prime ministership. Tony Abbott had just attempted to introduce a motion to suspend the former Speaker, Peter Slipper, and during his speech uttered the extraordinarily inflammatory phrase: 'Another day of shame for a government which should already have died of shame'.[11] Nothing could have been more calculated to upset and infuriate Gillard. This was the phrase that Alan Jones had used about her father. Now, just a few weeks later, weeks during which this language had been the subject of torrid discussion and debate, here was Tony Abbott using exactly the same words – to the Prime Minister's face. Gillard stood. She seemed to be quivering with rage. She fixed her eyes on the Leader of the Opposition.

'I will not be lectured about sexism and misogyny by this man. I will not.' Julia Gillard raised her hand and pointed her finger at Abbott. 'And the government will not be lectured about sexism and misogyny by this man. Not now, not ever.' She then went on to document 'the Opposition Leader's repulsive double standards, repulsive double standards' – she repeated the phrase – 'when it comes to sexism and misogyny'. She cited examples that were deadly in their impact. She gave an example of Mr Abbott questioning whether women are 'by physiology or temperament' less adapted to exercise authority than men. She quoted Mr Abbott, when referring to the carbon tax, as saying, 'What the housewives of Australia need to understand as they do the ironing...'. And she quoted Mr Abbott saying that she, Julia Gillard, needed to 'politically speaking, make an honest woman of herself'. This comment, Gillard pointed out, 'would never have been said to any man sitting in this chair'. Then she got really personal: 'I was offended when the Leader of the Opposition went outside in the front of Parliament and stood next to a sign that said, "Ditch the witch".' She went on: 'I was offended when the Leader of the Opposition stood next to a sign that described me as a man's bitch'. By the time she resumed her seat fifteen minutes later, Tony Abbott was cowering in his chair, looking ashen.

Gillard was at first oblivious to the impact she had had. When she sat down, she turned to Treasurer Wayne Swan and suggested she had better call for some correspondence to sign so she was not idle for the rest of Question Time. 'You don't follow a *J'Accuse* speech by signing letters,' Swan said to her. Anthony Albanese, the hard numbers man from the New South Wales Left who is also Leader of the House and Minister for Infrastructure and Transport, said that he actually felt sorry for Tony Abbott. 'For Anthony to feel sorry for a Tory,' Gillard said later at a private function, 'I knew I must have made an impact.' These comments by her colleagues provided Gillard with the first clue that she had done something remarkable. It was not long before the full impact of her words reverberated not just around the country but around the world. The ABC, which televises Question Time in federal parliament, put the speech[12] onto YouTube where it quickly went viral. More than 2,248,000 people had viewed it by early 2013, with most of these looking at it in the first few days. It was reported that there were 300,000 views in the first 24 hours. And the reaction was overwhelmingly positive. 'Australia's Prime Minister Julia Gillard is one badass motherfucker,' began a post on the American website *Jezebel.com*. It was headed: 'Best Thing You'll See All Day: Australia's Female Prime Minister Rips Misogynist, a New One in Epic Speech on Sexism'.[13] It was probably the first time Gillard had been called a 'badass motherfucker' and you got the sense she did not mind one little bit. Talk about cred.

Other international media were more sedate in their language, but no less praiseworthy. The speech 'amounted to a public shaming', reported the *International Herald*

Tribune.[14] 'This is one for the ages. Nobody has unmasked political hypocrisy with such fire, with such passion, in a long long time,' said an article headed 'The speech every woman should hear' and posted on the CNN website. 'The speech became a hit because of its raw eloquence and visceral emotion'.[15] Even *The New Yorker* ran a rave review on its blog: 'Supporters of President Obama, watching Gillard cut through the disingenuousness and feigned moral outrage of her opponent to call him out for his own personal prejudice, hypocrisy, and aversion to facts, might be wishing their man would take a lesson from Australia'.[16]

Political leaders from around the world praised Gillard for her fiery remarks. Barack Obama was aware of it, Gillard said a few weeks later after she had spoken with him by phone to congratulate him on his election victory. She also recounted that the President of France and the Prime Minister of Denmark (who happens to be a woman) told her how powerful they thought it was when they encountered her at the Asia–Europe meeting held in Laos in early November 2012. But perhaps the most poignant response came while Gillard was visiting India just two weeks after she delivered the speech. One of the Indian security guards assigned to protect her had watched the speech, Gillard said later, and was so moved by it that she asked if she could have her photograph taken with the Australian Prime Minister.

Only here in Australia did the speech get a sour response – from the media. The journalists of the Canberra press gallery, in particular, missed the point. 'We expected more of Gillard', screamed the *Sydney Morning Herald* the next morning. 'Julia Gillard confronted a stark choice yesterday – the political defence of her parliamentary numbers, or the defence of the principle of respect for women,' Peter Hartcher, the paper's political and international editor writer, wrote. 'She chose to defend her numbers. She chose power over principle. It was the wrong choice. It was an unprincipled decision and turned out not to be pragmatic either. The Prime Minister gained nothing and lost a great deal.'[17] Over at the *Australian Financial Review*, under the headline 'Gillard lets slip her chance to lead', veteran political writer Geoff Kitney wrote: 'Gillard spoke with such passion and, at times, venom about Tony Abbott's attitude to women that a whole lot of people who should have known better ignored the fact that she missed arguably the best chance of her prime ministership to appeal to the whole electorate rather than excite her feminist support base'.[18] Take that, Presidents Barack Obama and François Hollande.

The barrage was seemingly endless, especially from the right-wing side of the media landscape. Andrew Bolt called her 'a Greer-type gender warrior',[19] *The Australian* headlined an editorial 'Her gender or her judgment'[20] and that most reliable of knockers, Miranda Devine, ranted, 'as a woman I'm embarrassed, insulted and angry that the stocks of women in power have been brought so low. Playing the gender card is the pathetic last refuge of incompetents and everyone in the real world knows it.'[21] 'If you forgot the context, didn't overscrutinise the substance and just saw a powerful woman calling out sexism and saying she had had enough, it was arresting,' Lenore Taylor wrote.[22] Although Taylor conceded that Gillard had touched a nerve with women especially, even she could not recuse herself from the Press Gallery's groupthink: it was all about 'the context'.

That context was, the Canberra journalists decreed, former Speaker Peter Slipper's supposedly misogynist private text messages to a staffer. Tony Abbott had called for Parliament to condemn Slipper, and Gillard's speech had been in response to that call from Abbott. Although Gillard clearly said several times in her speech that she was 'offended' by Slipper's remarks, she was judged by the Press Gallery, by many others in the media and by the federal Opposition to have disregarded the context and to have made a calculated attempt to score cheap points by using 'the gender card'. You had to be in Canberra to see it that way. In fact, as Lenore Taylor correctly pointed out, 'The further away from the context people were, the more transfixed by the speech they seemed to be'. None of the newspapers ran Gillard's speech as their front-page lead the next day. That honour went to the resignation of Peter Slipper as Speaker, an event that occurred an hour or so after her speech and which, while of course significant, seemed hardly to rank in magnitude with a major prime ministerial slapdown of the Leader of the Opposition for being sexist and misogynist. The finger wagging by the media went on for weeks. A few non-Canberra commentators took contrary views: Graham Richardson, the former Labor minister and powerbroker who is now a political commentator wrote, 'She may well have saved her prime ministership'.[23] But mostly they hunted in their usual packs: 'Labor now moves forward from gender wars mistake,' said *The Australian* on 15 October 2012.[24] The *Australian Financial Review* went into a frenzy about misogyny:

> Ms Gillard's decision to accuse Mr Abbott of misogyny was based on political motives rather than any genuine grievance, and the debate has subsequently been hijacked by social media, radicals and our politically correct chattering class.
>
> Rather than using outlandish claims and Orwellian word manipulation to exaggerate differences between people, politicians and thought leaders should encourage all Australians to make the most of the abundant opportunities this privileged society provides, whatever their gender, race or social background.[25]

All of them missed the point. While the media was engaging in hysterical criticisms of Gillard, all around the world people were watching the speech with evident delight. Women and men, girls and boys. People of all ages and in all kinds of countries were unconcerned about the context. In fact they were probably quite puzzled at why the Australian Prime Minister had made these mystifying references to a Mr Slipper in the middle of her excoriating speech about sexism and misogyny. What was remarkable is that Gillard's comments about 'the context' did not deter a non-political or even a non-Australian audience from being transfixed by her remarks.

If, as Jane Caro put it,[26] my Newcastle speech 'hit a nerve and gave women the ammunition they needed', to confirm their gut feelings that Australia's first female Prime Minister was being badly mistreated, Gillard's speech provided the powerful personal dimension. Here was a woman saying, It has happened to me and I don't like it. But this was not just any woman. This was the Prime Minister, supposedly the most powerful woman in the country, saying 'I was offended'. She was telling us how she felt when she was called 'a bitch' and 'a witch'. She was not afraid to share her feelings with the world – and that was tremendously empowering for women everywhere. Most often, women in top jobs are loath to put themselves in such a position. Such women might be willing to denounce discrimination and sexism but, they are quick to reassure us, It's never happened to me. What nonsense. If you are an employed woman anywhere, but certainly in the western developed world, and you have to pour yourself into an outfit before you haul yourself off to the office, or wherever you work, each day, there is almost zero chance that you have not been patronised, been passed over for promotion, been paid less, had comments made about your appearance, had to put up with colleagues telling crude sexual jokes in your presence, or simply not been listened to when you spoke up at a meeting – because you are a woman. No woman is immune, be she a cleaner or a partner in a law firm (lawsuits tell us that, yes, even female partners working in large legal firms have been sexually harassed by their colleagues – and there are many more instances dealt with internally that are never the subject of lawsuits, or where the harassed woman simply leaves). We know of CEOs of large organisations who sexually harass staff members, and now we know that our Prime Minister has been similarly harassed by large numbers of her constituents.

For Gillard to stand up and say, *It has happened to me and I don't like it*, was a massive game-changer. She not only changed the conversation. She not only killed stone-dead the idea that a woman who complains of such things is a 'victim' and therefore to be either derided or pitied. She brushed aside with contempt the suggestion that speaking about one's experience as a woman is 'playing the gender card'. Abbott had said in response to her speech: 'Never, ever, will I attempt to say that as a man I have been the victim of powerful forces beyond my control and how dare any Prime Minister of Australia play the victim card.'[27] To which Gillard had replied: 'I think it is actually a manifestation of deep sexism that you would say that if a woman raises her voice then that is her playing the victim as opposed to her standing up for her rights'.

In documenting the vilification of Gillard in my New-castle speech I gave people ammunition. I gave them chapter and verse, examples of the disgusting things that were being said and the crude portrayals of her, which shocked and sickened most decent people. Gillard's speech did something even more potent. It gave other women permission to say, It's happened to me. Nothing could be more powerful. The oppressed suddenly standing up and saying: We are not going to take it any more. For a great many Australian women this was akin to a Rosa Parks moment in the history of women's equality in Australia. No more back of the bus or, in equivalent language, no more tolerating sexism and misogyny – in the workplace or anywhere else. Here women were standing their ground identifying sexism and saying: this has got to stop.

The response to her speech might have surprised Gillard, but she was quick to realise she suddenly had a whole new political repertoire at her disposal, one that she could uniquely employ. She would be able not just to paint herself in a new light, but she would be able to differentiate herself from Tony Abbott and he would find it awkward to respond.

In the weeks following the speech, Gillard attended a number of high-level women-only functions. The first was a dinner hosted by the law firm Minter Ellison in Canberra for around 120 women drawn from business and the public service. Gillard was interviewed after dinner, conversation-style, by ABC broadcaster Fran Kelly. I was not present but have spoken to a number of women who were there, not all of whom were fans, but who each enthusiastically described Gillard's performance as 'fantastic'. Gillard spent the entire conversation discussing what it was like to be a woman in her position. She said she did not like to complain about how she was treated because of the negative message it would send to younger women, but she did confide to the room that it was sometimes hard for her to get up in the morning to face the never-ending comments about her clothes and her appearance. When asked, Gillard said she thought that Tony Abbott was 'sexist', as were many of her Labor colleagues and other members of the federal Parliament.

Here was the most powerful woman in the land conceding that even she had to endure being treated differently, and less favourably, because of her sex. It was a grim concession, yet admitting it was also empowering. After her speech to Parliament, a lot of women said they had had two reactions. First, that it was now OK to talk about this stuff. If the Prime Minister could stand up and say she'd been treated this way, then so could every woman. They felt they were no longer victims; they were fighting back. The second reaction was: if it's happening to her, what must it be like for women with no power, for the low-paid and humble women who have no status and no means of fighting back? It became a moment of at least theoretical solidarity between privileged women and those with little power.

A few weeks later, Gillard attended a much smaller boardroom dinner at another law firm, this time in Sydney. The dinner was at Gilbert + Tobin and was hosted by partner Kate Harrison who had been a senior advisor to Gillard for the first year or so of her prime ministership. Again Gillard spoke frankly about what it was like to be a woman in the top job. She had changed. It was as if she had finally released her inner feminist. This was something many of us had hoped for since she had become Prime Minister. We were disappointed that she seemed reluctant to emphasise her sex. If anything, she went to pains to play it down. Even when addressing a feminist audience, such as when she delivered the Inaugural EMILY's List Oration in September 2012,[28] she had said: 'I never conceptualise my prime ministership around being the first woman to do this job. I conceptualise my job as being about delivering the things that make a difference for the nation'. She did go on to say that if her being in the job meant that 'even one woman or one girl sees a more expansive future, then it is worth it'. But she did not portray herself as a champion of her sex. Even when she had supported policies, such as paid parental leave or equal pay for community sector workers that would be of immense benefit to women, she played down the gender aspect.

Now, things were different. Gillard was now stressing her sex and she was standing up for women everywhere. She tweeted from the Asia-Europe meeting in Laos in early November that she was disappointed at how few of the leaders at the table were women. She did an unprecedented thing in a speech to the Business Council of Australia dinner in Sydney on 15 November 2012 and spelled out some of the policy initiatives her government was 'doing for women', as well as making the following, astonishing comment: 'I'm looking forward to seeing [gender equality] flow from the shop floor to the leadership level, where I'm sure that in a couple of years' time I won't still find myself meeting with boards where the only other woman is serving food'.[29] This was most definitely a new Julia Gillard. Here she was stepping into the inner recesses of sexism and misogyny in Australia. Even though the current and former chief executives of the Business Council of Australia are women, the overwhelming majority of its 100 members are men. This is a repository of corporate clout in Australia, an arena where few women have any power, and here was Australia's first female Prime Minister telling them she wanted it to change. I wish I had been there. I would love to have run my eyes around that room to watch the reactions of the men. Did they hear what she was saying? Did they take her seriously? Will Gillard, if she is re-elected in September this year, be sufficiently emboldened to follow the example of Norway and require these men to appoint women to at least 40 per cent of all board positions? If I were one of them, I would consider myself on notice.

In mid-December Gillard made another startling announcement. Her government announced it was now a priority to 'stop the barbaric practice of female genital mutilation in this country'.[30] Funds were to be provided, a summit would be held, laws would be reviewed and the cooperation of the states and territories sought. This was not the first time that a government had taken steps to try to address this terrible problem, but it was certainly the first time a prime minister had put her or his imprimatur on such a sensitive issue. The game had definitely changed. Was it just the speech that had done this? Or was the speech itself the result of a change of strategy? Had Gillard decided, or been advised, that it would be smart politics to start standing up for women?

I don't know the answer to this question, but I do know that during 2012 Gillard became increasingly close to Hillary Clinton and that they discussed these issues. Gillard could hardly have had a better role model. While she was Secretary of State, Hillary Clinton, made one of her priorities to 'ensure that women's issues are fully integrated in the formulation and conduct of U.S. foreign policy'.[31] For instance, she made it a requirement that every State Department desk officer had to know the fertility rate of the country they monitored. (She has also taken steps to ensure that women's issues remain a State Department priority even after her departure, according to *New York Times* writer Gail Collins.[32]) Being a champion for women and girls certainly did not do Clinton any political harm. She is one of the most admired women in the world and she is so popular in the United States that she could easily, if she chose, run for president in 2016. Perhaps Gillard has

observed this and decided to pick up a few pointers. Whatever the explanation, there is no doubt that the post-speech
Gillard has changed. She has been a powerful woman ready
to stand up for other women. And women love it.

In December, *Daily Life,* the Fairfax website directed
at women, invited its readers to nominate who should be
considered the most influential woman in Australia. Gillard topped the poll by a long margin and Sarah Oakes,
the editor, wrote it was due to the sexism and misogyny
speech. 'That Speech was the catalyst of many of the effu-
sive nominations Julia Gillard received to become Australia's Most Influential Female Voice,' she wrote. 'And while
it goes without saying that she is the most powerful person
in the country – we asked for a list of women who took a
strong, public stand on issues that are important to women
this year and our first female Prime Minister delivered.'[33]

The speech was 'a watershed moment for both the
Prime Minister and Australian women', said Oakes and
she was right. The Prime Minister not only stood up for
herself, she stood up for all women. She demonstrated the
power words have to help us understand our world – and
to transform it. We all know about the speeches that have
helped change history. The 1963 'I Have a Dream'[34] speech
of the Reverend Martin Luther King was one. We know
about speeches that have forced us to confront who we
are, such as the famous 1992 Redfern speech[35] by prime
minister Paul Keating that laid out what white people had
done to dispossess the original inhabitants of this land.

And, people were saying by the end of 2012, Julia's Gillard's 'sexism and misogyny' speech fell in that category of landmark speeches. After that speech, there would be no going back: for her, for women, or, we fervently hope, for the nation.

The reaction to my own more modest speech bore that out. First, there was the tremendous number of people who read it. By early 2013, an astonishing 105,000 people had come to my website to read it, including more than 10,000 who came the day after Gillard's speech. All up, there had been over 205,000 page views.[36] For a website that on a good day would get around 300 visitors, this was phenomenal. So many hundreds of people left comments at the bottom of the speech that we were forced to redesign the site; it could only accommodate eight pages of comments, but it attracted many more than that. What was striking about the comments was that, unlike the kinds of things you see posted on opinion websites on the ABC or attached to newspapers, only a tiny fraction of them were critical and none was abusive. I received none of the kind of sexist vituperative comments that I often get on Twitter.

By contrast, the comments posted under my speech mostly fell into two categories. There were those people, both women and men, who said they cried while reading it. It was enough to make you cry – with shame, with anger and with despair. I had a similar reaction when I first saw that awful image of the Prime Minister's face photoshopped onto the plump naked body. I was shocked, but it was not the kind of shock that comes with seeing a naked body; it was the shock of realising the depth of the hatred being directed at Julia Gillard. The people who left comments on my website were similarly overcome with shame at what was being done to our Prime Minister. I think they were experiencing a very natural and visceral reaction to the overwhelming evidence of misogyny. It is not pleasant to confront hatred. It is in fact pretty scary to realise that we women are, still, the targets of such twisted and bitter attitudes. It is, quite frankly, frightening, especially when you think about how many of our fellow citizens apparently feel this way and when you think how many actually disagree with the idea that women and men should be equal.

The second reaction was that people said they were glad that I had put into words and documented what they themselves had been noticing. People were picking up on the fact that the Prime Minister is not even accorded the respect of being addressed by her last name or title in the media and in formal situations. But people also said they were shocked by what I presented. Like me, when I first began the research, they had had no idea how bad it was. And very many people said they were pleased I had suggested an action: It stops me with me. Lots of people sent me emails saying they were taking this advice, and that gratified me greatly. Yet the letter that moved me most was sent to me as a private message on Facebook by a man I don't know. It was a confession, of sorts. He had been a party to circulating some of these vile emails, he told me. He had thought it was harmless, just a bit of fun. After he'd read my speech, he told me, he felt ashamed of himself and he wanted me to know that, from now on, It stopped with him.

Some months later, I was told of another action that in fact moved me to tears when I checked it out and found it to be true. On one of the vile anti-Gillard Facebook pages was the beautiful photograph of Governor-General Quentin Bryce and Julia Gillard, just after the former had sworn in the latter as Prime Minister. It was a great moment in Australian history and the photograph captured the warmth, as well as the solemnity, of the occasion. The person who administers this Facebook page posted this photograph on 15 March 2012 (almost two years after the day it was taken) and invited his followers to post comments in response to his question: What are they saying to each other? Dozens of people had posted nasty, offensive and, in many cases, disgusting comments involving lots of sexual suggestions. Then, on 7 September 2012, two days after my speech was posted on my website, a whole lot of new comments appeared under the photograph. It stops with me, they said. Ordinary people, women and men, decided to intervene and to challenge the sexism and misogyny that is so rife in this country and that was being used to denigrate our first female Prime Minister. Interestingly, the photograph and all the comments now appear to have been removed from the Facebook page, but this citizens' protest is captured forever, archived, in the Appendix to my speech, the one that contained material that was so truly awful that I decided not to show most of it when I presented my speech, but which I included, with suitable warnings, on my website.

I think that we are lucky to have a Prime Minister who has now decided to take up this fight. Julia Gillard is not dodging the responsibility to other women that comes from being the first woman to do the job. She was not cowed when the Leader of the Opposition said, as he did in parliament on the last sitting day of 2012, in reference to her famous speech: 'This is not about gender. This is about character and, Prime Minister, you have failed the character test.'[37] It is totally about gender. As I outlined in the previous chapter, Gillard is attacked in ways that would simply not be possible if she were male. Having our first woman Prime Minister has unleashed a veritable avalanche of sexism and misogyny. These attitudes pervade our culture. In many ways, they define us and they affect every Australian woman from the Prime Minister down. So let's stop fretting about our progress towards equality and start looking at barriers to success. And those barriers are, as the Prime Minister correctly called it: 'sexism and misogyny'. These are the real barriers to women achieving equality in Australia – which is why, we have finally decided, it has got to stop; which is why we are now 'destroying the joint'. We are destroying that old sexist, misogynist joint that would not let us in or, when it does, denies us legitimacy and treats us with disrespect and contempt.

Women are now standing up in protest and demanding an end to sexism and misogyny. The Prime Minister's
speech was one event that acted as a catalyst, but even without Gillard's dramatic intervention, there was a growing
sense of grievance and of women willing to take action in
ways that we have not seen since the 1970s. Women are
giving voice to their discontent. They are stroppy and
they want change. They are angry when they learn that
they get less than men do for doing the same job. They
turn out in their thousands to express their grief when a
young Melbourne ABC employee is raped and murdered.
They defiantly call themselves 'sluts' and march in protest
against sexist stereotyping. And the main sign that a new
movement is being born is the way women are again giving
voice to their irritation at everyday sexism. (There's even an
online movement, with its own Twitter account naturally –
#everydaysexism – where, in a modern form of conscious-
raising, women share their stories of the daily insults and
putdowns.)[38] It is often the little things that get you down,
that are the last straw. The everyday sexism project docu-
ments it all, in women's own voices. They might, as the
project's founder puts it, 'be serious or minor, outrageously
offensive or so niggling and normalised that you don't even
feel able to protest'. But, as a woman who posted to the
website in early February 2013 expressed it, 'for the first
time in thirty years of trying to call out incidents of sexism
I'm not being told to shut up, or that I'm the one with the
problem'.

There is a growing sense of solidarity and the growth of a movement. It is local, because that's where most of our issues are, but in the age of online interconnectedness, it is also global. Stories can be shared in seconds, protests and petitions can be organised and huge numbers mobilised. When Jyoti Singh Pandey, a physiotherapy student, was raped and beaten to death on a bus in India in December 2012, there was immediate international outrage from women. So too there was when we were moved to tears of anger when Malala Yousafzai, a brave young Pakistani girl, was shot in the face by the Taliban for daring to go to school. There's not a lot that we in faraway countries could do in practical terms, perhaps, except rage and mourn, but it was one more example of the outrage feeding into this growing movement of women's dissent and rejection of the misogyny factor.

Notes

CHAPTER 1

1. http://www.australianoftheyear.org.au/storage/8906_AOTY_history_booklet_internals_6.pdf
2. Indigenous women (and men) did not achieve suffrage at the federal level until 1962.
3. http://www.abc.net.au/news/thedrum/polls/ (Accessed 30 January 2013).
4. Anne Summers 'New criteria for Australia Day awards are in order', *The Drum* (ABC), 29 January 2013, http://www.abc.net.au/unleashed/4488154.html (Accessed 30 January 2013).
5. Martin Bonsey, *The Order of Australia Review 2011*, [Selected Sections] Government House, Canberra, June 2011, p. 21, http://www.gg.gov.au/sites/default/files/files/foi/OofAReview2011.pdf

CHAPTER 2

1. http://www.commondreams.org/cgi-bin/print.cgi?file=/news2005/0105-04.htm
2. http://www.voced.edu.au/content/ngv23001
3. Anne Summers, *The End of Equality: Work, Babies and Women's Choices in 21st-century Australia*, Random House, 2003. Also available as an e-book from the Random House website http://www.randomhouse.com.au/ebooks/
4. http://www.theage.com.au/articles/2004/05/14/1084289883805.html (Accessed 6 February 2013).

5.   http://www.fahcsia.gov.au/our-responsibilities/women/publications-
     articles/government-international/budget-publications/women-s-
     statement-2012-achievements-and-budget-measures

6.   Mark Davis, '2020 vision: Rudd summit to map future', *Sydney Morning
     Herald*, 4 February 2008, http://www.smh.com.au/news/national/2020-
     vision-rudd-summit-to-map-future/2008/02/03/1201973740462.html
     (Accessed 7 February 2013).

7.   See Anne Summers, 'The long hard road to reverse Howard's law', *Anne
     Summers Reports*, Number 1, November 2012, www.annesummers.com.
     au/asr/

8.   KPMG and ASX, *ASX Corporate Governance Council Principles and
     Recommendations on Diversity: Analysis of 31 December 2011 year end
     disclosures*, September 2012, http://www.asxgroup.com.au/media/asx_
     diversity_report.pdf

9.   http://www.asx.com.au/resources/listed-at-asx/gender-diversity.htm
     (Accessed 7 February 2013).

10. http://www.smartcompany.com.au/entrepreneurs/20110308-calls-for-
     quotas-for-female-directors-grow-as-survey-suggest-female-managers-
     better-than-men.html ; Joe Hockey, 'We need female quotas if all
     else fails', *The Australian*, 10 March 2011, http://www.theaustralian.
     com.au/opinion/we-need-female-quotas-if-all-else-fails/story-
     e6frg6zo-1226018634579 (Accessed 7 February 2013).

CHAPTER 3

1.   World Economic Forum, *Global Gender Gap Report 2012*, http://www.
     weforum.org/issues/global-gender-gap/

2.   Australian Bureau of Statistics, *Personal Safety Survey*, No. 4906.0 2006,
     p. 17, http://www.abs.gov.au/ausstats/abs@.nsf/mf/4906.0

3.   'Chief Commissioner Ken Lay speaks at the Royal Women's Hospital
     White Ribbon Day breakfast', 23 November 2012, http://www.
     vicpolicenews.com.au/our-say/10930-chief-commissioner-ken-lay-
     speaks-at-the-royal-womens-hospial-white-ribbon-day-breakfast.html

4.   Ben Schneiders, 'Domestic violence leave surges', *Sydney Morning Herald*,
     27 October 2012, http://www.smh.com.au/national/domestic-violence-
     leave-surges-20121026-28b9k.html

5.   Grattan Institute, *Game-changers. Economic Reform Priorities for Australia
     2012*, p. 38, http://grattan.edu.au/static/files/assets/ab2f7201/Game_
     Changers_Web.pdf

6.   http://stats.oecd.org/Index.aspx?DatasetCode=LFS_D

7.   http://www.abs.gov.au/ausstats/abs@.nsf/Lookup/by+Subject/4125.0-Ja
     n+2012-Main+Features-Labour+force-1110

NOTES TO PAGES 52–57

8. Hernan Cuervo and Johanna Wyn, 'Rethinking youth transitions in Australia: A historical and multidimensional approach', *Research Report 33*, Youth Research Centre, Melbourne Graduate School of Education, University of Melbourne, 2011, p. 40, http://web.education.unimelb.edu.au/yrc/linked_documents/RR33.pdf

9. Grattan Institute, *Game-changers*, p. 39.

10. Ibid., p. 38.

11. http://www.smh.com.au/opinion/editorial/a-180bn-reason-to-rethink-womens-work-20110828-1jgh8.html

12. http://www.pc.gov.au/research/staff-working/workforceparticipation (Accessed 17 March 2013).

13. AMP.NATSEM, *Income and Wealth Report, Smart Australians: Education and innovation in Australia*, Issue 32, October 2012, p. 32, http://media.corporate-ir.net/media_files/IROL/21/219073/AMP.NATSEM_32_Income_and_Wealth_Report_Smart_Australians.pdf

14. AMP.NATSEM, *Income and Wealth Report , She Works Hard for the Money. Australian women and the gender divide*, Issue 22, April 2009, http://www.natsem.canberra.edu.au/publications/?publication=ampnatsem-income-and-wealth-report-issue-22-she-works-hard-for-the-money

15. Ibid.

16. http://www.news.com.au/business/breaking-news/gen-x-women-drop-out-of-workforce-on-poor-health-job-security/story-e6frfkur-1225887848726

17. *The Integration of Women into the Economy*, Organisation for Economic Cooperation and Development, Paris, 1985, p. 76.

18. EOWA, *Gender Pay Statistics*, May 2012, http://www.wgea.gov.au/Information_Centres/Resource_Centre/Statistics/Gender_Pay_Gap_Fact_Sheet_May_2012.pdf

19. Glenda Korporaal, 'Hidden a gender: females get only 80pc of male pay', *The Australian*, 7 March 2012, p. 21, http://www.theaustralian.com.au/business/hidden-a-gender-females-get-only-80pc-of-male-pay/story-e6frg8zx-1226291144052

20. EOWA, *Gender Pay Statistics*, May 2012.

21. Ibid.

22. NATSEM, University of Canberra, *The impact of a sustained gender wage gap on the Australian economy*, Report to the Office for Women, Department of Family, Community Services, Housing and Indigenous Affairs, March 2010, p. v, http://www.natsem.canberra.edu.au/publications/?publication=the-impact-of-a-sustained-gender-wage-gap-on-the-australian-economy-1

23. Sue Dunlevy, 'Women lawyers not equal', *Daily Telegraph*, 12 August 2009, p. 3.

24. Graduate Careers Australia, *GradStats. Employment and Salary*

Outcomes of Recent Higher Education Graduates, December 2012, http://
www.graduatecareers.com.au/wp-content/uploads/2011/12/GCA-
GradStats-2012_FINAL1.pdf

25. http://www.graduatecareers.com.au/wp-content/uploads/2011/12/
GradStats-data-dispute-media-release-0401132.pdf

26. Catherine Fox, 'Gender pay gap is a zero sum game', *Australian Financial
Review*, 5 December 2012, http://www.afr.com/p/national/work_space/
gender_pay_gap_is_zero_sum_game_5lbPcU84LFy9hENFvj6sdO
(Accessed 7 February 2013). There is a lack of standardisation of many
of these figures. NAB's industry average figure (31 per cent) differs from
EOWA's (32.7 per cent).

27. *The impact of a sustained gender wage gap on the Australian economy*, p. vi.

28. Anne Summers, *The End of Equality*, p. 78.

29. http://www.theage.com.au/opinion/contributors/i-feel-like-a-million-
dollars-then-sex-rears-its-ugly-head-20130104-2c8sd.html

30. http://www.wgea.gov.au/Information_Centres/Media_Centre/Media_
Releases/271112_women_on_boards_but_not_leadership_pipeline.asp

31. Chief Executive Women and Bain & Company, *Creating a Positive Cycle:
Critical Steps to Achieving Gender Parity in Australia*, February 2013, p.
3, http://www.bain.com/Images/BAIN%20REPORT%20Creating%20
a%20positive%20cycle.pdf

32. http://www.apsc.gov.au/about-the-apsc/parliamentary/state-of-the-
service/new-sosr/06-diversity#women

33. In January 2013 the following women were Cabinet Ministers in the
Gillard government: Gillard herself; Nicola Roxon [on 2 February 2013
Roxon resigned from Cabinet], Attorney-General; Penny Wong, Minister
for Finance and Deregulation; Jenny Macklin, Minister for Families,
Housing, Community Services and Indigenous Affairs; and Tanya
Plibersek, Minister for Health. Female heads of federal government
departments were Jane Halton (Health and Aging), Lisa Paul
(Education, Employment and Workplace Relations), Kathryn Campbell
(Human Services) and Glenys Beauchamp (Regional Australia, Local
Government, Arts and Sport).

In March 2013, following the resignation of several ministers after an
abortive attempted coup against her leadership, Julia Gillard appointed
three women to the ministry: Jan McLucas, Sharon Bird and Catherine
King. These appointments, when added to the four women already in
Cabinet, brought the representation of women in the Gillard ministry
to a record 10, equalling one-third of the ministry. This was itself a
record for Australia and has rarely been equalled, let alone exceeded, in
other developed countries. At the time of writing, only France with an

equal number of women and men in the cabinet of Françoise Hollande, has total gender equity. In addition, one-third of the parliamentary secretaries appointed by Gillard are women, meaning the parliamentary leadership group comprises one-third women. By contrast, Tony Abbott's leadership team has only 18.75 per cent women: two out of a 20-member shadow cabinet, four in a 12-member ministry and just three of his 15 parliamentary secretaries.

34. Australian Human Rights Commission, *Our experiences in elevating the representation of women in leadership* (An initiative of the Male Champions of Change), 2011, http://humanrights.gov.au/sex_discrimination/publication/mcc/mcc2011.pdf The companies which signed up are: ANZ, Citi, Commonwealth Bank, Deloitte, Goldman Sachs, IBM, Qantas, Rio Tinto, Telstra and Woolworths Limited.

35. http://www.asxgroup.com.au/media/PDFs/20100630_changes_to_corporate_governance_principles.pdf

36. This one did: http://www.fairwork.gov.au/media-centre/media-releases/2012/02/pages/20120202-wongtas-penalty.aspx

37. Grattan Institute, *Game-Changers*, p. 45.

38. CBA, *Viewpoint*, No. 3, March 2011, p. 12. This issue seems to be no longer available for download. See press release that accompanied its release: http://www.commbank.com.au/about-us/news/media-releases/2011/150311-viewpoint-issue3-results.html

39. Adam Creighton, 'Broken puzzle of childcare', *The Weekend Australian*, 21–22 July 2012, p. 15.

40. *Many Australian families managing without childcare*, http://www.aifs.gov.au/institute/media/media120723.html

41. Emma-Kate Symons, private communication to author, July 2012.

42. Grattan Institute, *Game-Changers*, p. 43.

43. Emma-Kate Symons, private communication to author, July 2012.

44. National Press Club debate between Tanya Plibersek and Sharman Stone, 24 October 2007.

45. *Women & Super* website: http://www.womenandsuper.com.au/Essentials/SuperGenderGap (Accessed 20 January 2013).

CHAPTER 4

1. http://www.heraldsun.com.au/news/victoria/australians-not-sexist-towards-pm-says-independent-mp-bob-katter/story-fn7x8me2-1226263221969

2. The gender composition of all Australian parliaments is tracked and regularly updated by the Parliamentary Library in Canberra. Current tables can be seen at: http://www.aph.gov.au/About_Parliament/

Parliamentary_Departments/Parliamentary_Library/Browse_by_Topic/
women

3. http://www.state.gov/secretary/rm/2011/09/172605.htm (Accessed 22
July 2012).

4. Ibid.

5. http://annesummers.com.au/2011/02/finally/

6. http://parlinfo.aph.gov.au/parlInfo/download/media/pressrel/2207903/
upload_binary/2207903.pdf;fileType=application%2Fpdf

7. http://www.aph.gov.au/About_Parliament/Parliamentary_
Departments/Parliamentary_Library/Browse_by_Topic/~/media
/05%20About%20Parliament/54%20Parliamentary%20Depts
/544%20Parliamentary%20Library/Browse%20by%20topic/
Currentwomen.ashx

8. http://www.mamamia.com.au/social/julie-bishop/ (Accessed 26 January
2013).

9. There are 13 Liberal Party, 1 Country Liberal Party and no National
Party women in the House of Representatives, and in the Senate there are
6 Liberal Party women and 2 from the National Party; http://www.aph.
gov.au/About_Parliament/Parliamentary_Departments/Parliamentary_
Library/Browse_by_Topic/women

10. Farrah Tomazin, 'A gender neglected', *The Age*, 20 January 2013, http://
www.theage.com.au/opinion/politics/a-gender-neglected-20130119-
2d04g.html

11. http://www.companydirectors.com.au/Director-Resource-Centre/
Governance-and-Director-Issues/Board-Diversity/Statistics

12. Paul Bibby and Elizabeth Knight, 'In the majority already, it's a case of
merit over matter', *Sydney Morning Herald*, 9 March 2011.

13. http://www.asx.com.au/asx/research/companyInfo.
do?by=asxCode&asxCode=PBG

14. EOWA, *Australian Census of Women in Leadership 2012*, p. 15, http://
www.wgea.gov.au/Information_Centres/Resource_Centre/WGEA_
Publications/WGEA_Census/2012_Census/CENSUS%20REPORT_
Interactive.pdf

15. Ibid., p. 17.

16. Ibid., p. 21. A further seven women are chairs of companies that fall
outside the ASX 200, but are in the ASX 500. (As of February 2013.)

17. http://www.companydirectors.com.au/Director-Resource-Centre/
Governance-and-Director-Issues/Board-Diversity/Statistics and http://
www.womenonboards.org.au/pubs/bdi/2012/asx.htm

18. http://www.defence.gov.au/budget/12-13/pbs/2012-2013_Defence_
PBS_02_overview.pdf

19. See reference to 'More gender diversity protects women against sexism

and sexual harassment' in http://genderequity.ahri.com.au/docs/GEP-Building_a_Business_case_for_Diversity.pdf

20. 'Working without fear', http://www.humanrights.gov.au/
    sexualharassment/survey/

21. Ibid., p. 12.

22. Ibid., p. 58.

23. Ibid., p. 14.

24. Australian Human Rights Commission, 'Review of Treatment of
    Women in the Australian Defence Force, Phase 2 Report', 2012, http://
    humanrights.gov.au/defencereview/ADF_report/adf-complete.pdf

25. Mark Dodd and Ben Packham, 'Australian Defence Force to be set
    targets to recruit and promote more women', *The Australian*, 22 August
    2012. http://www.theaustralian.com.au/national-affairs/defence/
    women-cannot-and-will-not-flourish-in-the-adf-new-report-fears/story-
    e6frg8yo-1226455544586

26. The Phase 2 Report, 'Review into the Treatment of Women in the
    Australian Defence Force', p. 36.

27. AHRC's 2011, 'Report on the Review into the Treatment of Women in
    the Australian Defence Force Academy', p. 60.

28. Ibid., p. 59.

29. David Wroe, 'Rape suspects may be suspended by ADF while allegations
    assessed', *Sydney Morning Herald*, 14 January 2013, http://www.
    smh.com.au/national/rape-suspects-may-be-suspended-by-adf-while-
    allegations-assessed-20130113-2cnm5.html (Accessed 9 February 2013).

30. Ian McPhedran, 'Diggers killed while playing poker in tent', News.
    com.au, 5 September 2012, http://www.heraldsun.com.au/news/five-
    australian-soldiers-who-died-in-afghanistan-coming-home-on-raaf-c-17-
    transport-jet/story-e6frf7jo-1226464927075

31. Verona Burgess, 'What Smith didn't say', 'Canberra Insider',
    Australian Financial Review, 16 March 2012, http://www.
    afr.com/p/national/government_business/canberra_insider_
    J038ENAZVaNBcQUBQfPLJO (Accessed 9 Februry 2013) NOTE: this
    may be Paywalled.

32. Phillip Hudson, 'Federal politicians should be setting the example
    to the nation, says new parliamentary speaker Anna Burke', *Herald
    Sun,* 13 October 2012, http://www.heraldsun.com.au/news/national/
    federal-politicians-should-be-setting-the-example-for-the-nation-says-
    new-parliamentary-speaker-anna-burke/story-fncynkc6-1226494737993
    (Accessed 17 March 2013).

33. Lucy Clark, 'Anna Burke: Time to Rise Above', *The Hoopla*, 12 October
    2012, http://thehoopla.com.au/anna-burke-time-rise-above/ (Accessed
    17 March 2013).

CHAPTER 5 ·

1. Joe Aston, 'Sexist jokes served up at hotels association dinner', *Australian Financial Review*, 27 November 2012, http://www.afr.com/p/national/sexist_jokes_served_up_at_hotels_iWzLYGF2MY2nOHNQ7JXzTO (Accessed 31 January 2013).

2. The full speech can be found at http://annesummers.com.au/speeches/her-rights-at-work-r-rated/

3. The original R-rated version of the speech can be found at Ibid. Additional images, emails, etc. to those in the original speech and an appendix are at http://annesummers.com.au/her-rights-at-work-r-rated/newmaterial/

4. See for instance Geoff Kitney, 'Abbott gets hammered', *Australian Financial Review*, 21 August 2012, p. 6.

5. 'What Julia Told her Firm', *The Australian*, 22 August 2012, p. 11.

6. 'Julia clears the air as best she can', *The Australian*, 27 November 2012, p. 1; and 'Julia's First Duty of Care', *The Australian*, 27 November 2012, p. 11.

7. http://parlinfo.aph.gov.au/parlInfo/search/display/display.w3p;db=CHAMBER;id=chamber%2Fhansardr%2F2d5112d9-d29f-4121-aa4c-332814189972%2F0027;query=Id%3A%22chamber%2Fhansardr%2F2d5112d9-d29f-4121-aa4c-332814189972%2F0000%22

8. Anne Summers, 'The gender agenda', *The Sunday Age*, 26 February 2012, pp.11–12.

9. http://www.youtube.com/watch?v=ap0aPcstix0 first screened 16 November 2011.

10. http://www.digitalspy.com.au/tech/news/a410278/facebook-reaches-1-billion-users-worldwide.html

11. http://www.socialbakers.com/facebook-statistics/australia (Accessed 30 January 2012).

12. http://www.austlii.edu.au/au/legis/cth/consol_act/sda1984209/

13. http://www.austlii.edu.au/au/legis/cth/consol_act/sda1984209/s5.html

14. http://www.austlii.edu.au/au/legis/cth/consol_act/sda1984209/s14.html

15. http://www.news.com.au/top-stories/barren-gillard-unfit-to-be-pm/story-e6frfkp9-1111113448384#ixzz248ixawJX

16. Joe Kelly, 'Mark Latham says Julia Gillard Has No Empathy Because She Has No Children', *The Australian*, 4 April 2011; http://www.theaustralian.com.au/national-affairs/mark-latham-says-julia-gillard-has-no-empathy-because-shes-childless/story-fn59niix-1226033174177 (Accessed 23 August 2012).

17. Malcolm Farr, 'Tony Abbott tells Julia Gillard to "make an honest woman of herself" on carbon tax', *Herald Sun*, 25 February 2011;

http://www.news.com.au/national-old/tony-abbott-tells-julia-gillard-to-make-an-honest-womanof-herself-on-carbon-tax/story-e6frfkvr-1226012034629 (Accessed 1 September 2012).

18. Peter van Onselen, 'Backbench push for survival fuels leadership noise', *Weekend Australian*, 21–22 July 2012, p. 13.

19. Melissa Mack, '"Old cow" insult for PM Gillard', *InDaily*, 3 August 2012; http://www.indaily.com.au/?xml=mob&iid=66169#folio=1 (Accessed 23 August 2012).

20. *Trapman v. Sydney Water Corporation & Ors* [2011] FMCA 398 (2 June 2011).

21. http://www.austlii.edu.au/au/legis/cth/consol_act/sda1984209/s28a.html

22. For example, see the definition of 'sexual harassment' published by the Australian Human Rights Commission: http://www.hreoc.gov.au/sexualharassment/index.html

23. Patrick Durkin, 'Settlement in porn case', *Australian Financial Review*, 30 August 2012, p. 15.

24. Karl Quinn, 'Defiant Pickering says he's not finished with PM yet', *smh.com.au*, 24 August 2012, http://www.smh.com.au/opinion/political-news/defiant-pickering-says-hes-not-finished-with-pm-yet-20120823-24p11.html (Accessed 26 August 2012).

25. 'True, Sharon, but she is nippleless. Facebook will ban me if I draw nipples. It seems ok on indigenous birds tho. work that out', http://www.facebook.com/pages/Larry-Pickering/236991276355038?fref=ts

26. Emma A Jane, 'Your a Ugly, Whorish, Slut', *Feminist Media Studies*, 2012, DOI:10.1080/14680777.2012.741073, http://www.tandfonline.com/doi/abs/10.1080/14680777.2012.741073

27. http://www.comcare.gov.au/safety__and__prevention/health_and_safety_topics/bullying/Comcares_workplace_bullying_campaign

28. See, for example, *Damian O'Keefe v. Williams Muir's Pty Limited t/a Troy Williams The Good Guys* [2011] FWA 5311 and *Dover-Ray v. Real Insurance Pty Ltd* (2010) 204 IR 399; [2010] FWA 8544.

29. Anne Summers, 'It is Gillard's ability to connect with, surprise and delight a wide range of people that is her acc card', *The Age*, 26 June 2010, 'Insight', p. 3.

30. Phillip Coorey, 'Gillard Saves Labor', *Sydney Morning Herald*, 26 June 2010, http://www.smh.com.au/national/gillard-saves-labor-20100625-z9qy.html?autostart=1%22>first (Accessed 30 August 2012).

31. Barrie Cassidy, *The Party Thieves. The Real Story of the 2010 Election*, Melbourne University Press, 2010, p. 147.

32. See Table http://media.crikey.com.au/wp-content/uploads/2010/08/arthur.jpg

33. Barrie Cassidy, *op. cit.*, p. 163.

CHAPTER 6

1. http://www.pm.gov.au/press-office/addressing-gender-inequality-pacific (Accessed 3 February 2013).
2. Jane Caro, 'Why 2012 was a pivotal year for women', *Women's Agenda*, 20 December 2012, http://www.womensagenda.com.au/talking-about/opinions/jane-caro-why-2012-was-a-pivotal-year-for-women/201212191356 (Accessed 1 February 2013).
3. Antonia Raeburn, *The Militant Suffragettes*, Michael Joseph, London, 1973, p. 11.
4. http://www.facebook.com/DestroyTheJoint?fref=ts
5. Caro, 'Why 2012 was a pivotal year…'
6. http://www.abc.net.au/news/2012-08-23/pm-fires-back-as-australian-issues-apology/4218092
7. Jonathan Marshall and staff reporters, 'The PM's dad died of shame: Alan Jones under fire after cruel and offensive attack on Gillard', *News.com.au*, 30 September 2012, http://www.news.com.au/news/jones-says-gillards-dad-died-of-shame/story-fnehlez2-1226484826391
8. http://www.abc.net.au/mediawatch/transcripts/s3551607.htm
9. 'Macquarie suspends ads on Jones' show', *smh.com.au*, 7 October 2012, http://www.smh.com.au/entertainment/tv-and-radio/macquarie-suspends-ads-on-jones-show-20121007-27704.html (Accessed 1 February 2013).
10. Lara Sinclair, '2GB must weigh cost as big advertisers stay away from Alan Jones radio show', *The Australian*, 16 October 2012, http://www.theaustralian.com.au/media/broadcast/gb-must-weigh-cost-as-big-advertisers-stay-away-from-alan-jones-radio-show/story-fna045gd-1226496798017 (Accessed 1 February 2013).
11. Stephanie Gardiner, '"Died of shame": focus on Abbott's use of controversial phrase', *Sydney Morning Herald*, 10 October 2012, http://www.smh.com.au/opinion/political-news/died-of-shame-focus-on-abbotts-use-of-controversial-phrase-20121010-27cgd.html#ixzz2KC5Wkpdd
12. http://www.youtube.com/results?search_query=julia+gillard+misogyny+speech+abc&oq=Julia+Gillard+misogyn&gs_l=youtube.1.2.0l5j0i5.53832.61584.0.64324.21.15 (Accessed 1 February 2013).
13. http://jezebel.com/5950163/best-thing-youll-see-all-day-australias-female-prime-minister-rips-misogynist-a-new-one-in-epic-speech-on-sexism
14. Mark McDonald, 'Australian Leader Unleashes Blistering Speech', *IHT Rendezvous*, 11 October 2012, http://rendezvous.blogs.nytimes.com/2012/10/11/gillards-blistering-speech-a-model-for-obama/

(Accessed 3 February 2013).

15. Frida Ghitis, 'The speech every woman should hear', *CNN website*, 19 October 2012, http://edition.cnn.com/2012/10/18/opinion/ghitis-hypocrisy-womens-vote/index.html (Accessed 3 February 2013).

16. Amelia Lester, 'Ladylike: Julia Gillard's Misogyny Speech', *The New Yorker* blog, 9 October 2012, http://www.newyorker.com/online/blogs/newsdesk/2012/10/julia-gillards-misogyny-speech.html (Accessed 3 February 2013).

17. Peter Hartcher, 'We expected more of Gillard', *Sydney Morning Herald*, 10 October 2012, http://www.smh.com.au/opinion/politics/we-expected-more-of-gillard-20121009-27bd6.html#ixzz2JnfrqKgU (Accessed 3 February 2013).

18. Geoff Kitney, 'Gillard lets slip her chance to lead', *The Weekend Australian Financial Review*, 13–14 October 2012, p. 63, http://www.afr.com/p/opinion/gillard_lets_slip_her_chance_to_ Xq6YMQdEzMIDG5FsmqzuOO (Accessed 3 February 2013).

19. Andrew Bolt, 'Gillard's political hell is heaven for Kevin', *Daily Telegraph*, 18 October 2012.

20. 'Her gender or her judgment', *The Australian*, 12 October 2012, p. 15, http://www.theaustralian.com.au/opinion/editorials/her-gender-or-her-judgment/story-e6frg71x-1226493947829 (Accessed 3 February 2013).

21. Miranda Devine, 'Gender card is a loser', *Sunday Telegraph*, 14 October 2012, p. 41, http://www.dailytelegraph.com.au/news/opinion/miranda-devine-gender-card-is-a-loser/story-e6frezz0-1226494961475 (Accessed 3 February 2013).

22. Lenore Taylor, 'PM's speech did stir hearts', *Sydney Morning Herald,* 'News Review', 13–14 October 2012, p. 12, http://www.smh.com.au/opinion/politics/pms-speech-did-stir-hearts-but-remember-the-context-20121012-27i1h.html

23. Graham Richardson, 'Maxine, you're dead wrong about Julia planning to oust Kevin', *The Australian*, 30 October 2012, p. 12, http://www.theaustralian.com.au/opinion/columnists/maxine-youre-dead-wrong-about-julia-planning-to-oust-kevin/story-fnfenwor-1226505623136 (Accessed 3 February 2013).

24. 'Labor now moves forward from gender wars mistake', *The Australian*, 15 October 2012, p. 13, http://www.theaustralian.com.au/opinion/editorials/labor-now-moves-forward-from-gender-wars-mistake/story-e6frg71x-1226495707701 (Accessed 3 February 2013).

25. 'Australia is not misogynist', *Australian Financial Review*, 19 October 2012.

26. Jane Caro, 'Why 2012 was a pivotal year…'

27. Lenore Taylor, 'Is Abbott too "sexist" to rule?' *National Times*,

30 November 2012, http://www.smh.com.au/opinion/political-news/
is-abbott-too-sexist-to-rule-20121130-2ajx4.html (Accessed 3 February
2013).
28. http://www.pm.gov.au/press-office/inaugural-emilys-list-oration-
canberra (Accessed 3 February 2013).
29. Speech to Business Council of Australia dinner, 15 November 2012,
http://www.pm.gov.au/press-office/speech-business-council-australia-
dinner (Accessed 3 February 2013).
30. http://www.pm.gov.au/press-office/gillard-government-act-female-
genital-mutilation-australia (Accessed 3 February 2013).
31. http://www.state.gov/s/gwi/index.htm
32. Gail Collins, 'Hillary's Next Move', *New York Times*, 10 November
2012, http://www.nytimes.com/2012/11/11/opinion/sunday/collins-
hillarys-next-move.html?pagewanted=all (Accessed 3 February 2013).
33. Sarah Oakes, 'The 20 Most Influential Female Voices of 2012', *DailyLife*,
11 December 2012, http://www.dailylife.com.au/news-and-views/dl-
opinion/the-20-most-influential-female-voices-of-2012-20121210-2b55h.
html
34. http://www.youtube.com/watch?v=smEqnnklfYs
35. http://www.youtube.com/watch?v=mKhmTLN3Ddo
36. These figures are from tracking by Google Analytics.
37. Sid Maher and Pia Akerman, 'Tony Abbott will stay course on AWU',
The Australian, 30 November 2012, http://www.theaustralian.com.
au/news/investigations/tony-abbott-will-stay-course-on-awu/story-
fng5kxvh-1226527093509 (Accessed 3 February 2012).
38. http://www.everydaysexism.com/

Index